Brit Girls of the Sixties

Brit Girls of the Sixties

Dusty Springfield: Something Special

+

Helen Shapiro: Teenager Sings The Blues

David Bret

CONTENTS

ACKNOWLEDGEMENTS

W riting this book would not have been possible had it not been for the inspiration, criticism and love of that select group of individuals I regard as my true *famille et autre coeur*: Barbara, Irene Bevan, René Chevalier, Marlene Dietrich, Dorothy Squires, Roger Normand, *que vous dormez en paix*. Lucette Chevalier, Jacqueline Danno, Betty & Gerard Gamain, Annick Roux, Tony Griffin, Terry Sanderson, Helene Delavault, John & Anne Taylor, Axel Cotti, Caroline Clerc, Charley Marouani, David & Sally Bolt, and those *hiboux et amis de foutre* who happened along the way. And to Amália, always in my thoughts, Peter Burton, Chris Rogers...to my agent Guy Rose, and to my wife Jeanne, still the keeper of my soul.

David Bret, February 2010

Introduction

After Dorothy Squires and Gracie Fields, Dusty Springfield (1939-99) may well have been Britain's greatest female entertainer. She certainly was the one who made the biggest impression on the US market, with 18 singles in the *Billboard Hot 100*. The creator of the unique style known as "blue-eyed soul", she was possessed of a unique, malleable voice—flutelike, powerful, smoky and sensual, frequently in the space of the same song—and was instrumental in introducing Motown to Britain, where in 1964, 1965 and 1968 the *NME* voted her Top British Female Vocalist.

Following a lull in her career, she attempted a return to her former glory in her collaborations with the Pet Shop Boys, but the sheer mediocrity of the material when compared to that of her halycon days proved this to be short-lived. Other comebacks had been less successful: taken on by an American record company, she was given little or no choice in what she could sing—for a woman who put so much of herself into her work, a surefire recipe for disaster. Sadly, this very much larger than life lady succumbed to cancer, weeks short of her sixtieth birthday and on the very day that she would have received an OBE from the

Queen. Dusty remains a show business legend, despite the brevity of the central part of her career, yet she also remains an enigma, a completely self-fabricated, difficult yet strangely vulnerable woman who allowed few, if any, access into her complex, in turns exhuberant and neurotic world where there was at times little difference between reality and make-believe.

In an age where being gay or bisexual was tantamount to career suicide, Dusty fought tirelessly to keep her biggest secret, finally coming clean in the 1970s to Ray Connolly of London's *Evening Standard*: "A lot of people say I'm bent, and I've heard it so many times that I've almost learned to accept it...I couldn't stand to being thought of as a big butch lady. I know I'm perfectly capable of being swayed by a girl as by a boy. More and more people feel that way, so why shouldn't I?" And that was it—all that fuss over nothing. She was, after all, still the same Dusty.

Chapter One

Where Am I Going?

S he was born Mary Isabel Catherine Bernadette O'Brien on 16 April 1939, in a West Hampstead nursing home, and into a relatively well-off but not entirely stable family. Her tax accountant father, Gerard, had been born and raised in India, but shunted back and forth to Derbyshire for his education. Her mother, Kay (Catherine Anne Ryle) hailed from Dublin, but had been brought up in Tralee. From an early age, Kay had nurtured aspirations to go into the theatre. In 1927, aged 25, she had relocated to London to hopefully realise this ambition, and had at once been indoctrinated into the flapper set. Flappers were radical young things, very much in the stamp of the *demi-mondaines* of turn-of-the-century Paris. They lived life to the full, drank spirits and smoked cigars or cigarettes when it was considered vulgar for women to do so, insulted their peers, painted their lips bright red, bobbed their hair, and casually used "in words" such as "divine", "shit" and "darling". They shocked their mothers, guardians and maiden aunts by shedding their inhibitions and their corsets. A young woman who wore her stays publicly was referred to as "Old Ironsides", and no self-respecting flapper would dream of hanging on to her virginity past the age of twenty. Dusty Springfield would inherit many of these traits from her mother.

Needless to say there were fireworks when word of Kay's activities reached her staunchly Catholic parents: though well into her twenties when her father ordered her to ditch her "dirty" life and start searching for a suitable husband, she dared not oppose him, though it had taken her until the age of thirty-one to settle for shy and retiring Scotsman Gerard O'Brien, five years her junior and the very antithesis of the loud, anything-goes Kay. Neither was it by all accounts a happy union. Like many ex-Colonials, OB as he was more familiarly known had had it bred into him that a woman's place was in the home, and that she should follow the rules he installed within that home. This discipline, accompanied by physical violence, would subsequently be exercised over his family—the O'Brien's had a son, Dion, born in 1934—and frequently involve application of OB's belt or the back of his hand. Even so there were the lighter moments, such as the occasional musical soiree

when the O'Briens gathered around the piano—with the classically-trained OB, or child prodigy Dion tinkling the ivories and Mary playing the "maraccas" courtesy of a box of dried peas—to entertain the neighbours, who earlier in the day may have been treated to one of their frequent rows, which at their most vociferous could be heard at the other end of the street. In August 1985—though this was not the real reason for her remaining single—Dusty told Jean Rook of the *Daily Express*:

> You want to know why I'm not married? I suppose because my parents didn't get on. My father was an income tax consultant who wanted to be a concert pianist—a very bitter men with a foul temper. By the time I was at school my mother thought he was repulsive. I can't remember a thing about my room at home except the raised voices coming from the next door room—the intense bitterness. I'd feel embarrassed

to go out with my parents because the arguments
still continued. I never invited friends home
because I cringed about the rows. I thought, if I
married, I would repeat their performance.

Home for the O'Brien's at the time of Mary's birth was a
five-floor house at 97 Lauderdale Mansions, though they moved
around so often over the course of the next few years that it
becomes near impossible to keep track: from the no less opulent
Sumatra Road, in Maida Vale, to the basement of a public house
in High Wycombe to escape the horrors of the Blitz, then back to
the hustle-bustle of London. And eternally rowing, surviving a
hellish marriage not uncommon to many of their generation. It
was a case of one making one's bed and lying on it, with divorce
never being an option no matter how dire the circumstances
unless one wished to be regarded as the family or parish pariah.
For the rest of their lives, Gerard and Kay O'Brien would fight
and throw things at each other, but never quite get around to
calling it quits.

From an early age, Mary O'Brien acquired the name
"Dusty"—it is believed on account of her then tightly-curled red
hair and her tomboyish mien which in school photographs reveals
her looking exceedingly butch, a far cry from the beautiful,
sophisticated creature a few years down the line. Much of her
childhood was spent cowering in her brother's shadow. Dion was
the firm family favourite and could do no wrong: good-looking,
robust, bright and confident whilst she was dumpy, plain and
bespectacled, and prone to every childhood ailment. Whilst he
was praised for the slightest achievement, she was persistently
reminded that she would never be as good as him, instilling
within her an instability—and some reckoned an element of self-
loathing—which remained with her for the rest of her life. As
such, in adulthood she would frequently recount wildly
contrasting versions of the same anecdote which neverless always
pointed to the fact that she had been a desperately unhappy child.

There were also far too many childhood bumps and bruises, and the question must be asked as to how many of these were genuine accidents, and how many the result of parental or self-abuse. She certainly seem to have gone out of her way to gain her parents' affection. "Because I was so unhappy as a kid," she told Jean Rook in August 1985, "I used to go into corner and cling to the hot water pipes in my bedroom until they were cold, to prove I really existed." She also very strongly believed in the theory that the apple rarely fell far from the tree, telling the *Evening Standard*'s Ray Connolly on the eve of her thirtieth birthday, "I don't know whether whether I want children or not. The urge to reproduce is always there, of course, but then I think 'what for?'. I probably wouldn't be a good mother. It would be great spasmodic moods of affection which don't last."

Dusty also maintained that she had never once seen her parents hug or kiss. Little wonder then that she grew up despising many, trusting few—a tetchy, difficult woman always on her guard, terrified of letting go and revealing her true self. Like David Bowie, Dalida (of whom more later) and Morrissey, Dusty Springfield completely reinvented herself, weaving a web of fantasies, half-truths and foibles about her persona so that by the end of the process it becomes impossible to separate the real person from the self-fabricated creation. Throughout her life she constantly switched identities: the creation which as Dusty Springfield craved attention and adoration from behind the footlights, only to retreat once the curtain came down behind the Garboesque facade of Mary O'Brien, the shy creature who went to inordinate lengths to protect the true identity she did not wish the world to see.

The fantasies, daydreams and distractions evolved from Dusty's fascination with glitzy, exotic high-camp Hollywood musicals starring the likes of Carmen Miranda and Maria Montez, vulnerable gay icons of a earlier generation whose tragic lives had been played out in full Pirandelloesque public glare. One day, she would augment their ranks, becoming along with Judy, Piaf, Marlene and Marilyn one of the great gay icons of the twentieth century. Unaffected by the war—she was only a few months old when it started it, six years old when peace was declared—she was not musically enamoured of Forces favourites Vera Lynn and Anne Shelton, as has been stated. Her earliest memories, extant of Miranda and Montez, were of blonde glamour girls June Haver, Betty Grable, and Doris Day. Having inherited her mother's longing to tread the boards, such thoughts clouded her concentration much of the time during her school years. In September 1944 she was enrolled at The Sands Catholic Primary (later St Augustine's) in High Wycombe. In those days, parts of the Buckinghamshire town were a veritable League of Nations: thousands of Irish, Jamaicans, Trinidadians and Poles had settled here to fill vacancies by those men who had left to fight in the war. Needless to say, racial prejudice ran high, though not so far as Dusty was concerned. Her ex-Colonial father may have looked down his nose at some of these people and dismissed them as underlings, but integrating with such a colourful, joyful crowd introduced Dusty to the black culture she would come to revere as an integral and essential component of her musical sphere.

Because she spent so much time with her head in the clouds, Dusty's parents never expected her to pass her Eleven-plus examination—Dion was a pupil at the town's Royal Grammar—but she did, and in September 1950 moved to St Bernard's Convent School, a charitable institution run by the Daughters of Jesus, and where the Mother Superior was an eccentric lady who smoked a clay pipe. She stayed here until the end of 1951, when the O'Briens returned to London.

Home for the next few years would be West Ealing's Kent Gardens, and a much tougher school when Dusty was enrolled at St Anne's Convent, a private establishment run by thee Sisters of Charity of St Jeanne-Antide. Here, she suffered the penance of a personal path to Calvary. She was made to recite the Catechism every day, and to attend Confession at least once a week—rapped over the knuckles with a ruler by the nuns, and mocked by the other girls if she had no culpabilities to confess, so much so that she began inventing them just to fit in. And whilst other schools hired charabancs to take their pupils to the seaside, St Anne's organised "political and debating" outings to the House of Commons, or "punitive" trips to Lourdes where, upon threat of excommunication, the girls were instructed to stay away from the opposite sex. To add to her suffering, it was around this time that Dusty became aware of her sexuality, which must have made life unbearable in this over-chaste environment where she never ceased to be reminded of what hell would be like unless she lived an impossibly blemish-free existence. Her secretary, Pat Rhodes, later stated that in her opinion, Dusty actually felt guilty about her sexuality because this went against the teachings of the Church—that to better cope with her inner demons, she became a lapsed Catholic.

At St Anne's, music once more became Dusty's solace, though like sex, unless this involved singing hymns the subject had to be discussed in darkened corners, out of earshot of the nuns. In these days she had a palpable crush on Peggy Lee, who she first saw in a remake of *The Jazz Singer* with Danny Thomas in 1952. Blonde, beautiful and sophisticated, Peggy remains alongside Ella Fitzgerald one of the finest American song stylists to have drawn breath. Her big numbers in the film were Rodgers and Hart's "Lover" and Cole Porter's "Just One Of Those Things", but Dusty "flipped her lid" over lesser-known gems such as Peggy's own composition, "Where Can I Go Without You?" A few years from now, Dusty would copy her idol by bleaching her blonde locks and dropping her voice half a tone (the back-combing would come later still) to sound more like her. Though she once somewhat foolishly boasted that she had achieved greater success than her idol, this was untrue: Peggy Lee had fifteen years of career behind her when Dusty discovered her, and would have a good fifteen more after Dusty had passed her prime. No such songs were on the agenda, however, when she formed a group with two schoolfriends, Jean MacDonald and Angela Patton: singing at friends' houses or at the school on feast days, their set included blues standards from the Billie Holiday and Bessie Smith repertoires, which the nuns frowned upon to such an extent that the trio folded after a couple of months.

Inasmuch as Dusty had surprised her family by passing her Eleven-plus, so she did so again by acquiring four O-levels: English Grammar, French, Geography and History. Despite this, her parents' praise was reserved for Dion, who had just turned twenty-one and landed a well-paid job as a bank clerk. Whenever Dusty addressed visitors to Kent Gardens in accentuated French, Kay or Gerard would remind them that, whatever their daughter had just said, their son could pronounce it better and in *nine* languages. She breathed a huge sigh of relief when, in July 1955, she passed through the gates of St Anne's for the last time. Reasonably well-qualified, she could have pursued any number of career paths, but instead chose to go on the stage. She enrolled with the Jane Campbell Acting Class, a local repertory group whose speciality was Method and mime. Unable to cope with "psyching" herself up for a role, or being told to open a door when there was no door there, after just two weeks she threw in the towel and got a job in a laundry. The early hours here did not suit her, and after less than a month she packed this in and found a position with Bentall's department store. She was fired from here when, whilst filling in for an absent colleague in the toy department, a customer asked her to demonstrate a model railway and she blew every fuse in the building.

Taking a job in a record shop, Dusty developed another crush—on pretty blonde Irish songstress Joan Regan, who had had big hits with "Ricochet" and "If I Give My Heart To You". She saw Regan at the Hackney Empire, and whilst she disliked her longish hair—grown so to advertise Drene shampoo on the television—she loved her flouncy, hooped dresses with their many petticoats. She also went to see Eve Boswell and Lita Roza—the latter wore a slinky , hip-hugging purple sheath-dress. Setting a valuable precedent, Dusty went to Harrod's sale and spent a whole week's wages on one such creation. She put this on in the privacy of her bedroom, grabbed a hairbrush, and used this as an imaginary microphone to mime the latest Peggy Lee and

Joan Regan hits in front of the mirror. Encouraged by Kay and Gerard to broaden his musical horizons—they were not so enthusiastic when it came to supporting their daughter's formative career—Dion had recently begun singing folk songs and could be found most evenings performing in the clubs around Sloane Square. His seemingly limitless talents filled Dusty with both jealousy and envy, but she tagged along and in doing so found an outlet for her own introverted talents—introverted because, thus far at home and at school, no matter what she did she was persistently put down. "I used to get very upset that I wasn't good enough," she told the *Daily Mail's* Chrissy Iley in 1990, "The feelings of inadequacy followed me through my life. Now, I'm grateful to my brother because it was he who unwittingly started me off singing. I started because he started, and I wanted to be better than him at *something*."

Time would prove this to be so. Closing her eyes and pretending that she was back in her bedroom, Dusty began singing one evening in the dressing room and was overheard by the manager: he suggested that she transfer her talent to the stage, the audience liked her, and she left the club with a clutch of bookings for this and other clubs in the area. Her new vocation as a *chanteuse* was however to be short-lived. For one thing, her father made a nuisance of himself, turning up unannounced every evening to ensure that she was behaving herself and not drinking. For another, not content with emulating Doris Day, Joan Regan, Lita Roza and Ruby Murray, she began singing obscure Latin numbers which resulted in audiences chatting loudly whilst she was on stage. This became so bad that the manager paid her up and she left the club in floods of tears, vowing never to face a microphone again. Disillusioned, she continued working at the department store.

So far as her parents were concerned, Dusty's clubland failure was a blessing in disguise. Such places were only hives of temptation: the demon drink, and predatory men. In fact, she seems to have been interested in neither. "Men were mysterious objects rather than people you love, and with who you feel comfortable, so I went in for crushes rather than involvement," she later told *Woman* magazine. She was still at heart a good Catholic girl who believed that sex before marriage was wrong, and as Kay O'Brien had once seriously considered having her daughter groomed for holy orders, there was not much chance of her being encouraged to fall in love. What Kay had not reckoned with, of course, was the safer bet of being attracted to other girls in that she she would never suffer the indignity and shame of falling pregnant.

Salvation came in the form of a singer named Iris Long, aka Riss Chantelle, a former guitarist with the all-female Ivy Benson Band. Along with Lynne Abrams, Chantelle had formed The Lana Sisters: hoping to become the next Beverley or Kaye Sisters, they had placed an advertisement in *The Stage* for a third contralto member. Dusty replied, claiming that she was resident singer at a piano bar near Victoria Station. Fortunately for her, Chantelle never checked her credentials: Dusty was one of a dozen girls interviewed, and fit the bill perfectly. The appointment coincided with the O'Brien's relocation to Brighton, and offered Dusty the perfect opportunity to put some space between them—she moved in with Lynne Abrams, who lived with her parents in Hertford.

Dusty's tenure with The Lana Sisters would be brief, but moderately successful. The trio were part-handled by Eve Taylor, Adam Faith's manager and the future Svengali of Sandie Shaw— a tetchy, difficult individual loathed by her discoveries, but tolerated because she pulled out all the stoppers to get her acts noticed. One of the trio's first engagements was sharing the bill with 18-year-old Faith at the 2i's Coffee Bar, which stood at 59 Old Compton Street (now occupied by the Boulevard Bar) in the heart of Soho. "The club was the fuse for the UK rock and roll explosion," Faith recalled, "A little ground floor cafe with linoleum floors and formica tables, and a battered piano. Everyone expected it to be a nine-day wonder, but all those old-timer agents sitting around in their old timer restaurants, shaking their heads and saying it wouldn't last, they were all proved wrong." When Dusty met Adam Faith, a London film-cutter with a curious "hiccuping glottal" voice, he was fronting a skiffle group, The Worried Men, at the 2i's. After releasing a clutch of failed singles he would temporarily abandon his music career and return to being Terry Nelhams, film-cutter, though his and Dusty's paths would soon cross again.

Soon after hiring Dusty, The Lana Sisters signed a record deal with Philip's subsidiary label, Fontana, and released their debut single, "Chimes Of Arcady", c/w Brenda Lee's "Ring-A-My-Phone". The A-side, written back in 1930 by American ragtime composer Percy Wenrith, had most recently provided a hit for Billy Vaughan. The record got nowhere, but it did lead to an appearance on *6.5 Special*, the UK's very first television magazine for teenagers, founded by Josephine Douglas and Jack Gold and launched in February 1957. Hosted by Pete Murray from the BBC's Riverside Studios, it had gone out with the kitschy introduction, "Welcome aboard the *6.5 Special*. We've got almost a hundred cats jumping here, some real cool characters to give us the gas". So, let's get on with it and have a ball!" The Lana Sisters opened the show for some of the big names of the day: Cliff Richard, Johnny Ray, Morecambe & Wise, Mike & Bernie Winters, Slim Whitman, even Nat King Cole. They harmonised well and looked good in their spray-on lamé pants, though they were not a patch on The Beverley Sisters, with whom they were most often compared. For their one-off performance on *6.5 Special* they sang "Buzzin'", of which the least said the better. During the Spring of 1959, Eve Taylor also secured them a spot on the BBC's shortlived *Drumbeat*, alongside the recently returned Adam Faith. Whereas he performed the bouncy, "What Do You Want?", which would rocket to the top of the charts, they opted for the more sophisticated Continental sound, singing their cover version of Italian star Mina's million-selling "Tintarella Di Luna", which they released as a single early in 1960. It was good, but did not sell.

In all, The Lana Sisters released seven singles , including "A Heart Divided", with up and coming jazz-stylist Kenny Colman. They *almost* made the big time when they recorded "Seven Little Girls Sitting In The Back Seat", a catchy number which had almost taken Paul Evans & The Curls to the top of the US *Billboard* chart. Sadly, in the UK the girls were pipped to the post by The Avons, whose cover-version proved one of the year's biggest and some thought most annoying hits. In December 1959, performing this song, The Lana Sisters guested in Tommy Steele's Christmas specatcular. Effectively, this was Dusty's swansong with the trio, who soon afterwards were voted seventh in the *Melody Maker*'s Top British Vocal Group category. Even after little less than a year with Riss Chantelle and Lynne Abrams, she was convinced that she had much more to offer the entertainment world than a handful of novelty numbers and meaningless little ditties. And she, who had despised her brother Dion for monopolising her parents' attention and affection, now turned to him to move her one step closer to her goal.

Chapter Two

The Springfields: Island of Dreams

Since leaving school, Dion O'Brien had like his sister changed jobs several times. After leaving Lloyds Bank, he had tried his hand at stockbroking, and had eventually joined the Royal Artillery who had subsequently assigned him to the Intelligence Corps as a Russian interpreter. Upon his discharge in 1958, at around the time Dusty joined The Lana Sisters, Tom Springfield—as he was now calling himself—also launched himself on the music scene as as half of a duo, The Kensington Squares. Tom's singing partner was Tim Feild, an ex-Etonian who had served with the Royal Navy: upon his discharge, it has to be said with financial support from his wealthy family, had hitch-hiked and busked for a whole year across most of the Far East and America. The same age as Tom, as Reshad Feild he would later carve his niche as an acclaimed spiritual teacher and author. The Kensington Squares had soon established themselves on the London folk scene, benefiting from Feilds' travelling experience and Tom's expertise in languages to become a kind of multinational Kingston Trio.

The decision to add a female vocalist to their line-up and follow in the footsteps of The Mudlarks and The Weavers occurred when The Kensington Squares and The Lana Sisters were performing at different venues in Taunton, Somerset. Tom and Feild put the proposition to Dusty, who said that she would think about it: she did not want to leave Riss Chantelle and Lynne Abrams in the lurch. Also she had reservations about spending too much time with Tom, who had not been her favourite person in the world when they had both been living at home, with Tom getting all the praise whilst she had often been treated like a nonentity. "I felt awful about leaving them," she later said, "I kept thinking that they thought I had only used them for experience—though sometimes you *have* to let people down in order to get on."

Needless to say, the parting of the ways was acrimonious, albeit a necessary one for Dusty, whose musical tastes were far more in keeping with her brother's than those of The Lana Sisters. With Lynn Abrams moving on to other ventures, a few years later Riss Chantelle formed The Chantelles with Sandra Orr and Jay Adams, releasing their debut single, "I Want That Boy", on Parlophone in 1965. Three years later, they disbanded.

How the name The Springfields came about is not known. Dusty often half-joked that their first rehearsal had taken place in a field on a sunny Spring afternoon. Other sources that, glancing at a map of America, Tom commented on how many Springfields there were dotted around—alternatively, that the monicker was the brainchild of their eccentric Welsh manager, Emlyn Griffiths, who emulated comedian Fred Emney by dressing like a toff and wearing a monocle. Griffiths' first move was to book them on a summer tour of the Butlins holiday camps, on a combined salary of £50 a week, along with whatever tips they could make. For four months they travelled up and down the country in a clapped-out Volkswagen camper van, frequently breaking down and hitching lifts from truck drivers to get them and their equipment to their destination. Much of the time their reception was mixed, primarily because they never quite knew what to sing—folk, pop, Latin or Continental. Their attempts to inject a little sophistication into the proceedings by throwing in the odd

Russian, French or Hebrew phrase failed miserably—this was not what was required during "Pit Week" in Filey! The youngsters in the audience screamed for Tommy Steele and Cliff Richard, while their parents demanded David Whitfield and Ruby Murray. What they got was "old ham" such as "Goodnight Irene" and "Joshua Fit The Battle Of Jericho"—and they showed their appreciation by chattering loudly whenever the trio were on the stage.

By the autumn of 1960, and the close of the holiday season, The Springfields were ready to play to more appreciative audiences. Emlyn Griffiths landed them on their feet, so to speak, by booking them for a four-weeks season at The Churchill Club, a society watering-hole in London's Mayfair. Here, performing their unique brand of pop-folk which ranged from American campfire ditties and Continental favourites, they were in their element and proved so popular with the mostly upper-crust clientele that their run was extended four times. Thenon the trio accepted temporary demotion, performing on packed variety bills, often as the warm-up act whilst the audience were still talking their seats. They persevered, and in the end their patience paid off when, in April 1961, they were approached by Philips Records' Johnny Franz and offered an audition for a recording contract.

Johnny Franz (1922-77) was a hugely successful record producer who almost exclusively specialised in home-grown talent mostly not even interested in conquering the fickle American market. A former office boy in London's Denmark Street—with its music shops and publishers, clubs and street-musicians the British equivalent of Tin Pan Alley—he had gone on to become a club pianist, then a pianist with the legendary George Shearing before moving to Philips in 1954, whence he had accompanied Anne Shelton and produced her chart-topping "Lay Down Your Arms", famously adding the soldier's marching sound by getting an assistant to shake a box of frozen peas! Franz had also produced for Frankie Vaughan, Susan Maughan, Marty Wilde, and a very young Shirley Bassey. Later he would triumph with The Walker Brothers, and of course with Dusty's solo ventures.

For their audition, The Springfields performed some of the material from their Churchill Club programme: mostly American folksy numbers such as "Gotta Travel On", "Far Away Places", and "Dear John", Tom's tongue-in-cheek arrangement of the Civil War Anthem, "Marching Through Georgia". The latter had Dusty coming in with a solo refrain, emulating a coquettish Southern belle, and it was this song that Johnny Franz decided would be their debut single. Rush-released in May 1961, the record did not chart, but it received sufficient airplay on the BBC's Light Programme—in pre-Independent days, the UK's only easy-listening radio station—to put The Springfields on the map. Shortly after releasing their second single, "Breakaway", their names figured amongst the *New Musical Express*'s "Ten Future Attractions" list—a not so very accurate forecast, for of the others only "Moon River" singer Danny Williams would amount to anything.

"Breakaway" just managed to scrape into the UK Top 30, and led to The Springfields being offered a tour with comedian Charlie Drake. They also performed live on the Light Programme's *Saturday Club* and *Easy Beat*, and guested on television's top-rating *The Benny Hill Show*. Their "third-time lucky" single, released in time for the 1961 Christmas market, was "Bambino", a seasonal song, sung in English and Italian. The Springfields' record company boasted that it would rival the song of the same name, released four years earlier by Franco-Italian star Dalida. This was expecting a lot. It reached Number 16 in the charts, but it was not a patch on the Dalida song—which topped the French charts for a staggering 45 weeks, a record which has never been broken.

Dalida (1933-87), though always more popular than Dusty, was her nearest European equivalent. Dusty favoured covering American hits, Dalida English ones, with both stars making their own property whatever they covered, no matter who had sung them first. Both completely reinvented themselves and,

chameleonlike, changed their images each passing season—
Dalida started out as the plain and frumpy Yiolande Gigliotti and
within a year had transformed herself into a beautiful but very
insecure swan. Like Dusty she would prove impossible to handle
at times, in her case driving one husband and two lovers to
suicide. Like Dusty she was too fragile, too vulnerable to cope
with her monstrous success. Like Dusty she would make
numerous attempts to take her own life, and eventually succeed.
Later in Dusty's career, her manager Vic Billings would make
repeated demands on her to work with Dalida, as Petula Clark
did, but her plans would always fall through at the last moment—
such a shame, for together they would have been electrifying.
And it was Dalida, ahead of Cliff Richard, who dubbed Dusty
"Le Négresse Blanche"—The White Negress, an appellation she
wore with great pride, once telling a journalist, never more
seriously, "I wish I'd been born black!"

"Bambino" could have paved the way for a Continental
career, such as the one currently being enjoyed by Petula Clark
and Richard Anthony. On the B-side of their next single, the
tiresome "Goodnight Irene", The Springfields were singing of
"Far away places with strange-sounding names," whilst aside
from a visit to Ireland with The Lana Sisters, Dusty had never
been out of the country. Philips, however, were interested only in
cracking the much more lucrative American market—once, that
is, the trio had finished promoting their recently released debut
album, *Kinda Folksy*.

Though popular with fans and a collector's item today—
ahead of their "great project" The Springfields look wholesome
as apple-pie on the cover, with a purple-clad Dusty sitting on
front of a conga drum—the album was a confusing mish-mash,
harking back to their recent holiday camps tour when, unable to
categorise themselves, they had been unsure what to sing for
couldn't-care-less audiences. The harmonising is mostly
uneven—the men shout as if in competition with each other to
drown out Dusty completely, and some songs are way too heavy
on the bongos and conga drum. Unsure whether fans would want

to go the whole hog and fork out for the 12-inch, Philips issued the twelve tracks on three 7-inch EPs. The album kicks off with "Wimoweh Mambo"—noisy and cluttered, performed way too fast, and positively awful when compared with the superlative (and phenemonally popular) versions by Yma Sumac and Karl Denver. Things improve considerably with "The Black Hills Of Dakota", from Doris Day's hit movie, *Calamity Jane*, only to degenerate again with the corny "Row, Row, Row". "The Greenleaves Of Summer", Dimitri Tiomkin's sublime theme from *The Alamo* (performed over the credits by The Kingston Trio) offers a few minutes of magnificence before mediocrity beckons once more with "Silver Dollar" and Irving Gordons "Allentown Jail". Joe Stafford had introduced the latter in 1951, and if her version was not the definitive one, the more recent French version by Edith Piaf certainly was—Dusty herself admitted this. Next up is a way over the top "Lonesome Traveller", followed by a very pleasing "Dear Hearts And Gentle People. Sammy Fain had composed this for Bing Crosby, and it is with this type of cosy fireside number that The Springfields truly excelled. "They Took John Away" and "Two Brothers", a hammy Civil War song, are scarcely worthy of mention. The album ends on a lamentable note with Olavi Virta's "Eso Es El Amor", and the trio's mauling of "Tzena, Tzena, Tzena", Issachar Miron's Yiddish anthem which The Weavers & Gordon Jenkins had recently performed so well.

As had happened with The Lana Sisters, the novelty of working with a trio—of not being completely independent—soon started to wear off when Dusty realised that The Springfields were not heading in the direction she had hoped for. For one thing, their tastes in music were different. Whereas as Tom and Feild leaned towards the exotic—the maxim being, "Why learn to speak nine languages if these can't be incorporated into the act?"—Dusty was becoming increasingly magnetised to the black sounds winging their way across the Atlantic. Peggy Lee, Doris Day et all had been shunted aside in her emotions to make way for obscure (at that precise moment in Britain) R & B acts such as The Marvelettes and The Shirelles, all-girl groups from the relatively new Tamla-Motown label, founded in 1958 by a 29-year-old black entrepreneur named Berry Gordy.

Though no one suspected it at the time, the Motown explosion would be massive: what set out with Gordy borrowing $800 from his family to set him up in business would become a multi-million dollar empire and give the world Martha & The Vandellas, The Supremes, The Four Tops, Stevie Wonder, and a host of others. The Marvellettes would enjoy nineteen *Billboard* Top 40 hits in eight years, beginning in 1961 with "Please Mr Postman", a catchy little ditty which had nevertheless taken five people to write it. The Shirelles, the first all-girl group to have a US Number On—their "Soldier Boy" knocked Elvis' "Good Luck Charm" off the top of the charts in 1962—had formed at around the same time as The Lana Sisters. Dusty would have been far happier recording covers of their B-sides than some of the material chosen by Tom Springfield, and this almost certainly contributed towards some of the dissention between them. One only has to study the British charts to see what the record buying public wanted: Cliff Richard, Helen Shapiro, Adam Faith, Elvis, Billy Fury and Shirley Bassey were riding the crest of an immensely popular wave, and they were not doing this with tosh like "Swahili Papa".

Effectively, Dusty's final emulation of Peggy Lee was to copy her bobbed, blonde hair—firstly by dying her own locks exactly the same shade, then by buying a succession of wigs. Some biographers, focusing much of their attention on the negative aspects of Dusty's life, have stated that she effected the change because of self-loathing, the fact that she hated the image which stared back at her in the mirror, but this it not true. Like many Catholic girls (and boys too, if one studies Morrissey's case) who questioned the more profound ethics of their faith, she simply needed some means of alleviating the enforced drudgery of a religion which had taught her every fear known to mankind. "The more I watched myself on the then black-and-white television, the more alarmed I became," she said later, "In monochrome, my red hair looked jet black. It had to go!" The bobbed hairstyle would give way to the beehive wigs which would make her appear much taller than her 5 feet 2 inches. It was also at this time that she officially became known as Dusty Springfield, though she had been using the name for some time.

Additionally, there were the well-publicised personality clashes. Dusty, as yet still a minor star, bore all the traces of a prima donna in the making. She refused to handle the suitcases which contained her hooped, multi-layered stage dresses. What else were men for but to fetch and carry for the lady? Similarly, Tom and Tim Feild felt that they were entitled to a little male bonding—therfore if there was substantial time to wait between trains, Dusty was left baby-sitting the trio's luggage and equipment in the crowded waiting room o draughty station hall whilst they headed for the nearest bar. There were also heated arguments about television shows, and Dusty's attempts to draw attention to herself not just by dying her hair, but by "hogging" the camera—something she could not help, for she had always stood between the two men, face-on, as happened with all two male-one female acts. As if to get even for this, Tom also exluded her from press interviews. "It was this machismo thing," she told journalist Kris Kirk, "I was expected to go on stage and sing my little old heart out, and for the rest of the time keep my mouth shut and my opinions to myself."

Dusty's singing voice was fairly strong—not super-charged in the Bassey-Squires sense, but exceptionally controlled in the upper register. Her major problem was that she was performing with two men who, on the face of it, were flat and tuneless shouters as opposed to singers. As such, as a result of trying to keep up with them, early in 1962 she was hospitalised for several days with severe throat strain. Effectively, the only break she had from this was when The Springfields were appearing on television—for pop groups promoting their latest release, miming was almost always the order of the day until this was outlawed in 1966. And miming was something Dusty had problems at the best of times—again, like Dalida, some of her lip-synching in filmed clips is dire, and this caused backstage tension. Additionally, there were rows about society status. Dusty had always considered herself middle class, but accepted the fact that, in this new helter-skelter world of pop, amendments had to be made to one's lifestyle: cheap transport between engagements, tawdry guest-houses with shared bathrooms, meals snatched here and there. This Dusty was willing to accept, and to a certain extent so was Tom. Tim Feild, however, does not appear to have wanted to compromise. He came from a wealthy background, and had always been accustomed to the best things in life. Backstreet lodging houses, roadside cafés and greasy spoons were not his style.

The Springfields also had to deal with press speculation that Dusty and the married Feild were having an affair. To a certain extent, Dusty played along with this. The world was yet to discover that she was gay, and in any case she was too busy forging ahead with her career to pay much attention to her love life.

In the May, The Springfields came one step closer to making that all important trip across the Atlantic when they released "Silver Threads And Golden Needles", Dick Reynolds and Jack Rhodes' bluegrass classic which in future years would be performed by artistes as diverse as Brenda Lee, Dolly Parton and Janis Joplin. The Springfields' reading of the song is by far the best version of all, and is delivered in the "country-rock" style later championed by Gram Parsons. The record (along with its successor, the dreadful "Swahili Papa") bombed in Britain, but topped the Australasian charts. More importantly, issued on the Mercury label, it shot into the *Billboard* Top Twenty. The single was followed by an album of the same name, which all sold phenomenally well.

Immediately there were calls for trio to record and tour Stateside. This time the move was curbed by escalating problems within The Springfields' camp. In the July, shortly after cutting "Swahili Papa", Tim Feild announced that he was leaving. The official reason was that his wife was seriously ill, and he needed to look after her. Unofficially, Feild is said to have been sick of getting caught up in the middle of the O'Brien siblings' escalating quarrels. He did however agree to hang on until Tom, always the mastermind between major decisions, had found a replacement. As had happened with The Lana Sisters, an advertisement was placed in *The Stage*, and auditions were held in whichever town The Springfields were appearing—currently they were supporting Bobby Vee. In Coventry, Tom interviewed an old friend, Michael Longhurst-Pickworth, a 21-year-old singer-songwriter-guitarist who had also been a friend of Eddie Cochran. The two had appeared on Jack Good's television showcase, *Oh Boy!*. For Dusty, this was too much of an omen: the "Summertime Blues" singer had been travelling through Wiltshire in a taxi on 16 April 1960, Dusty's twenty-first birthday, when it had crashed into a lamp-post. Cochran, critically injured, had died the next day, himself aged just twenty-one. Soon aftewards, Mike Hurst as he would subsequently call himself, had given up the music business and taken a job selling insurance. Now, he was coaxed back into the limelight, much to Dusty's dismay. Said her later secretary, Pat Rhodes, "He was very abrasive....his manner was brash and he didn't blend in so well. When Tim left, the warmth of the music disappeared."

Mike Hurst's first studio work as a Springfield was the session which produced *Christmas With The Springfields*, a four-track EP which, unusually, was given away free with *Woman's Own* in December 1962. Much more important was the subsequent session which include "Island Of Dreams". Tom's own composition and arguably their most celebrated song, they recorded it in October 1962, coupled with the cowboy ditty, "The Johnson Boys". Dusty often confessed to disliking it, saying, "I wince every time I hear it!" Cynics (and wishful thinkers) have suggested that this was on account of its opening stanza, "I wander the streets and the gay crowded places,"—-particularly a generation later when the word "gay" had a different meaning, when there was speculation that the phrase alluded to "cruising" for sex, which is not true. A catchy, optimistic piece, it opens after a brief harmonica solo and with its for once perfect harmonising and irregular choral backing immediately uplifts the listener, though as happens with many groups (The Smiths and Morrissey, Queen and Freddie Mercury), one's attention is at once drawn to the frontman (or woman!)—in this case Dusty, whereas the other members of the ensemble find themslelves relegated to the minor key. The lyrics also bring to the fore the Americanisms she had picked up while listening to her favourite black music, which would crowd her output for the rest of her career—the "*hah in the skaa*" for "high in the sky". The song was immensely popular: it reached Number 5 in the British charts, and stayed in the Top Thirty for almost six months. When the figures were tallied at the end of 1963, only The Beatles had outsold The Springfields.

Coming from the same session as "Island Of Dreams" was Tom and Clive Westlake's "Little Boat", which The Springfields were asked to perform in *Just For Fun*, directed by Gordon Flemyng. An enjoyable piece of tosh billed as "*the* big teen musical", this tells of a bunch of teenages' quest to win the vote, and is worth seein for the wealth of pop talent from Britain, America and France: familiar names Bobby Vee, Mark Wynter, Kenny Lynch, The Crickets, Johnny Tillotson and Ketty Lester, whilst representing the French *yé-yé* wave were Eddie Mitchell, Richard Anthony, and Sylvie Vartan—the latter, along with Dusty, being the only one who is as much a household name today as she was back then.

Whilst "Island Of Dreams" was still riding high in the charts, Philips were appoached by Shelby Singleton, since 1956 the A&R man-turned-producer with Mercury, the company's US sideshoot which operated from Nasheville, Tennessee. An aficionado of black music, Sheldon had produced Brook Benton's "Bol Weevil Song", which had reached Number 2 in the *Billboard* chart in 1962. Since then he had enjoyed great success with Roger Miller and Jerry Lee Lewis—in 1969 he would buy out Sun Records along with its rock and roll back catalogue. Though not a great fan of their music—he had heard

The Springfields in London the previous year, but not expressed any desire to meet or sign them then—as would happed with Nana Mouskouri and French rocker Johhny Hallyday (during his formative years, married to Sylvie Vartan) he recognised a neat little money earner when he saw one, and invited the trio to record their next album, *Folk Songs From The Hills,* at his studio.

The Springfields arrived in Nashville just before Christmas, blithely unaware of the working methods here. In England they had recorded only those songs they liked, the ones which had been "proved" on the tour circuit. Admittedly some of their choices had been poor, but at least they had had a say in the matter. In Nashville, they were instructed to turn up at the studio first thing, where they were handed the sheet music for that day's song which they would be expected to learn, rehearse and record by the end of that day's session. This went on for four weks. Additionally, they had to contend with surly technicians who resented any artiste who was not home-grown, and insulted by musicians who spent most of the time yelling instead of talking. On the plus side, they got to perform in a few of the smaller clubs, and on local radio.

One gets the impression today that someone was taking The Springfields for a ride by getting them to record *Folk Songs From The Hills*. Just what was Shelby Singleton thinking about! Dusty sounds so out of place here that she becomes frequently embarrassing to listen to, through no fault of her own forced into attempting to sound connvincing in a dozen songs which would not have been out of place in *The Beverly Hillbillies* television series. "Greenback Dollar" and "Foggy Mountaintop" are passable, but everything else is instantly forgetable, and should be when compared to Dusty's later work. Even the album cover is patronising: Dusty, wearing a tartan dress, sits on a straw bale while the men, dressed in striped "humbug" jackets pose behind her with banjo and guitar.

There was to be a positive aspect of Dusty's first trip to the United States. During a brief stopover in New York, she found time to go shopping—always a favourite passtime—not for clothes, but for records of black artistes not yet readily available in British shops. In September 1985 she would tell our mutual acquaintance, *Gay Times'* Kris Kirk, of the revelation which occurred one afternoon while she was strolling past a Times Square record shop:

> The Exciters' *Tell Him* was blasting out. The *attack* init! It was the most exciting thing I'd ever heard. The only black music I'd heard in England was big-band jazz and Latin music which I loved. But this was a revelation. I copied a lot of black music, though I'd say The Exciters and The Shirelles influenced me more than Motown. But I'd copy them all! One day I woke up wanting to be Dionne Warwick, the next day The Ronettes. It took me some time to find my own style.....

The Exciters (formerly The Marvelettes) were an all-girl-group, a one-hit wonder whose catchy Leiber & Stoller tune reached Number 4 in the *Billboard* chart shortly after The Springfields returned to England. Dusty would one day call lead singer Brenda Reid and thank her for providing her with the catalyst she had needed to turn solo. "When Dusty talked about this group," Kris Kirk told me, "Her eyes lit up like a child who's just discovered she's the sole occupant of Santa's grotto. 'That day,' she said, 'I well and truly saw the light!'"

The seed had been sown for Dusty to branch out on her own, and at exactly the right moment. From a commercial point of view—and money was all that mattered with *every* record company—folksy outfits such as The Springfields were becoming old-hat. In January 1963 when the trio returned home, The Beatles, heading the Liverpool Invasion, were riding high in the British charts with their second single, "Please Please Me". Other big names, the ones who would not last as major stars, but who made their impression while they were here included Brian Poole & The Tremeloes, Gerry & The Pacemakers, Billy J

Kramer & The Dakotas—and The Rolling Stones, who would outlast everyone.

Prior to the pop world taking the full force of this explosion, The Springfields recorded "Say I Won't Be There", Tom's take, in no way related to the original, of "Au claire de la lune". The trio performed it on Alan Freeman's *Here Come The Girls* television show, though the attention—hence the title—was more focused on Dusty than on her colleagues. In France, France Inter's José Artur played it on his late night radio show with the erroneous announcement, "And now, here's the latest offering from Dusty Springfield." The writing was very definitely on the wall, despite successful lightning tours of Australasia and Europe. To coincide with their dates in Germany, they released an EP containing a German language adaptation of "Island Of Dreams", but radio stations refused to play it because it included Pete Seeger's "Sag mir wo die Blumen sind"—this was already regarded as Marlene Dietrich's

personal property. In the March, Dusty made her first official "solo" appearance on the panel of the BBC's *Juke Box Jury*, hosted by David Jacobs. "Suddenly, Dusty is emerging as an interesting personality," observed the *New Musical Express*. On 3 July, The Springfields appeared in a command performance before the Queen, at Glasgow's Alhambra Theatre. Topping the bill was Connie Francis. The press reported the trio to be earning in excess of £1,500 a week, a tidy sum for the time.

On 4 October, Dusty was co-presenter on television's latest teenage pop magazine, *Ready, Steady, Go!* Conceived by Rediffusion's Elkan Allen and produce-manager Vicki Wickham, this was especially geared towards the Mods, who flaunted their latest fashion trends each Friday evening following the show's logo, *"The weekend starts here!"* *RSG*, as it was familiarly known, ran between August 1963 and December 1966. It's regular hosts were Keith Fordyce, and "groovy chick" Cathy McGowan who transformed giggly, fawning presenting almost into an art form. Topping the bill in this show were The Beatles, and initially the interview went well when she asked Paul

McCartney, "Is it true that you sleep with your eyes open?" Then,through no fault of her own (she was reading the questions from the sheet of paper given to her by the producer) with her clipped accent and shy mien Dusty made a pig's ear of her interview with the forthright, somewhat crude John Lennon. Firstly she asked him if the rumours were true that he had once been shot for scrumping apples. When he affirmed this, she wanted to know if the pock-marks on his face were the result of his injuries. "No," he drawled, "They're scabs!" Lennon then asked to see Dusty's scabs, bringing their pointless repartee to a premature conclusion. "I think this is where we'd better finish," she murmured, "What are you going to sing next?" Thankfully, her next two interviews for the show were less embarrassing.

In the meantime, The Springfields were pencilled in for the Royal Variety Show, on 4 November at London's Prince of Wales Theatre: topping the bill would be Marlene Dietrich, with The Beatles halfway down the pecking order. When producer Val Parnell replaced them in this show with Tommy Steele, to compensate he offered them a spot on *Sunday Night At The London Palladium*, broadcast live on 6 October.

Effectively, this would be The Springfields' swansong. They received a standing ovation after "Island Of Dreams", then Dusty announced that after tonight, the trio would be disbanding. There was an audible gasp from fans in the audience, while those watching at home were equally shocked, though the backstage rumours had persisted for several months. What everyone found bizarre was their farewell number: Woodrie Guthrie's "So Long, It's Been Good To Know You". This was hardly sentimental stuff—a "corn-on-the-cob ditty" about moving home to avoid a dust-storm—but halfway through, Dusty burst into tears. Later she claimed that, like a drowning man whose life flashes before his eyes, in the space of a few seconds she had contemplated a very uncertain future. As will be seen, she had gone to great lengths to stage the event, and the crocodile tears were her way of putting The Springfields behind her so that she could get on with planning the career she knew she merited.

Chapter Three

La Négresse Blanche

D usty's brother Tom claimed that the reason for The Springfields' split was that *he* had forecast the staggering success of The Beatles, with whom no group would ever be able to compete. Therefore it had been preferable to disband while they were ahead. The music press made up their own minds, citing personality clashes. Some years later, Dusty told an Australian journalist, "A group is an open prison. After a while you get tired of living and working with the same people, and being disciplined at the same time from outside." She had recently been singled out from the trio and voted Britain's 8th most popular singer in a *Melody Maker* poll, and since the emphasis had been on her for some time, it now seemed prudent that she should want to spread her wings.

Tom went on to become a record producer and, courtesy of his sister who introduced them, a songwriter for The Seekers. His compositions for them included "A World Of Our Own" and "The Carnival Is Over", by and large better than anything he had written for The Springfields. With actor co-writer Jim Dale he received an Oscar nomination for "Georgie Girl", and during the late Sixties released two solo albums. Today, he is most remembered for his work with the Australian group, and for being Dusty Springfield's sister. Mike Hurst fared considerably better. After a short-lived tenure with The Methods, he began producing for Andrew Oldham and Mickie Most, and discovered Cat Stevens. Amongst the big names he produced were The Troggs, Spencer Davis, and Manfred Mann.

To launch her solo career, Dusty had no shortage of helpers. Absent-minded and unable to do most things for herself, she acquired a secretary-cum-factotum: Pat Barnett (later Rhodes), had worked for Emlyn Griffiths. Johnny Franz agreed to be her record producer, and she appointed Vic Billings as her manager. Billings, a tough-talking but with Dusty a gently persuasive man, had formerly booked variety acts for London's New Victoria Theatre before being appointed deputy controller of bandleader Victor Sylvester's dance studios. Currently, he had a small stable of artistes which included Eden Kane, and Paul Raven, who later achieved notoriety as Gary Glitter. Billings would later describe Dusty as the most pessimistic optimist he had ever known—clipping only the bad reviews of her work, and ignoring the good ones—but he would stick with her through thick and thin. He was one of the few people (along with Pat Rhodes and Johnny Franz) capable of calming her down when she was in one of her moods. Ivor Raymond (1926-90), an actor-musician who had worked with The Springfields and appeared in *Hancock's Half Hour*, and who was currently employed by the BBC as a musical director, was asked to provide her with a song. Collaborating with Mike Hawker, who had written "Walking Back To Happiness" for Helen Shapiro, he came up with "I Only Want To Be With You". The number was completed in a single evening in Raymonde's office at the BBC, and sung to Dusty down the phone at seven the next morning. Or so the press were led to believe.

In fact, the whole process was a charade. Dusty had contacted Billings during the summer of 1963 and a few weeks later Johnny Franz, unbeknown to Tom Springfield and Mike Hurst, had agreed to produce her debut single, which she wanted to be a Bacharach-David song. These two were currently the rage in

America. Missouri-born Bacharach had been collaborating with David since 1957, while doubling as Marlene Dietrich's orchestra leader. Their first big hits had been "The Story Of My Life", which had become British singer Michael Holliday's signature tune, and the Perry Como hit, "Magic Moments". More importantly so far as Dusty was concerned, the two had written for rising Motown star Dionne Warwick, who they had employed to pitch their work to other artistes until Bacharach, a master of uneven phrasing which adapted well to her unusual voice, had realised that she performed them better herself. He was not, however, currently interested in composing for Dusty Springfield: Marlene disliked her (though she would soon revise her opinion) because of The Springfields' German language version of "Where Have All The Flowers Gone?" Dusty therefore focused her attention on the Ivor Raymonde song which she recorded, along with "Once Upon A Time"—not at the end of October as publicised, but on 27 September at the Olympic Sound Studios, nine days *before* The Springfields' split. The next day he had played the finished result to Johnny Franz and Vic Billings—with Tom and Hurst still unaware of what was happening—and within the hour Billings had given instructions for Dusty's name to be added to the playbills for his Pop Extravaganza tour, about to hit the road. She would be sharing equal-billing with Dave Berry & The Cruisers, The Searchers, Brian Poole & The Tremeloes, and Freddie & The Dreamers.

The charade continued when, at the eleventh hour, The Springfields were added to the line-up of *It's All Over Town*, a pop quota-quickie directed by Douglas Hickox. Like *Just For Fun*, this was another slice of hokum aimed at promoting the pop stars of the day and selling their records. Co-written by Lance Percival, who headed the credits, the cast included Frankie Vaughan, The Bachelors, The Hollies, and Clodagh Rogers. The film's musical director just happened to be Ivor Raymonde, which gave he and Dusty plenty of opportrnities to huddle in corners and discuss her future without anyone getting suspicious. The Springfields sang both sides of their new single, now the only promotion this would get—"If I Was Down And Out", c/w "Maracabamba", a monstrosity even more dreadful than their take on "Wimoweh". This would be released in January 1964, and not surprisingly prove a flop.

For her first solo outing, Dusty had asked Johnny Franz to duplicate Phil Spector's trademark "Wall of Sound" production technique, a multi-layered, dense but slightly tinny effect which sounded especially good on jukeboxes, but which on account of the technical wizardry involved did not reproduce well on the stage. Spector specialised in black girl-groups, The Ronettes and The Crystals being his biggest success story so far. Dusty was looking for an orchestral backing along the lines of The Crystals' "Then He Kissed Me". Ivor Raymonde had recorded the orchestrations at the Marble Arch Studios on 23 September, using twenty members of The Royal Philharmonic. He had then slightly distorted the acetate to come up with a near-replica of the Spector sound, at a fraction of the cost. A pleasing cacophony of cascading drumrolls, horns and rock guitars, and with an elaborate string-filled middle-section solo, "I Only Want To Be With You" was released on 8 November 1963. With Dusty's own composition, "Once Upon A Time", on the flipside it reached Number 4 in the British charts, and peaked at Number 12 on the US *Billboard* chart, quickly earning her a gold disc for sales in excess of a million copies. Unlike most of the early Spector recordings, almost half a century on it does not sound dated, and has fuelled many cover versions ranging from a passable one by Annie Lennox, to a truly lamentable one by *Sun* Page Three Girl, Samantha Fox.

Because she had been a last minute addition to Vic Billings' tour, Dusty had no backing group, therefore when the tour kicked off in Halifax she was accompanied by The Cruisers. These were able musicians, well-suited to Dave Berry's plaintive vocalising, but what Dusty really needed was "oomph"—an ensemble which would provide her with the ersatz Motown sound she championed. This lack of cohesion robbed her early live solo performances of their magic, and affected her nerves which were never strong at the best of times. She had always suffered from stagefright, but whilst with The Lana Sisters and The Springfields there had always been someone else on stage to guide her through her set. Standing in front of a quartet of strangers made her terrified of forgetting her words, and at the back of her mind was the dreading that audiences would laugh at her. This never happened, but each evening ended with her in a bad mood, taking her frustration out of whoever happened to be close at hand— more often than not, Vic Billings.

It was Billings who placed the newspaper advertisements this time, though to be honest, it was unfair of him to have added her to the tour in the first place without the requisite musicians. Eventually, after several auditions she settled for The Echoes, who joined the tour in Liverpool shortly before Christmas. Formed in 1959 as Chris Wayne & The Echoes, the group had worked with Conway Twitty, Gene Vincent, and Jerry Lee Lewis. After several changes, their line-up when they joined Dusty was bassist Douggie Reece, organist Micky Garrett, Peter Clifford on guitar, and Bob Wackett on percussion. Later, The Echoes ranks would be swelled by the addition of trombonist Derek Wadsworth, trumpeter Derek Andrews, and numerous black backing singers. "The only ones worth having," she said. Her favourite was Madeleine Bell, an aficionado of the great gospel singer Mahalia Jackson who had arrived in Britain in 1962, aged twenty, with the *Black Nativity* gospel revue. Written by gay radical Langston Hughes, this had played on Broadway before touring North America. When Dusty met Madeleine Bell the revue was playing to packed audiences at the Strand Theatre: when it closed and the rest of the troupe headed home, Bell stayed put. Though she was always kindness itself to her backing singers, she could be an indisputable martinet where her musicians were concerned, yelling and screaming abuse of they messed up an arrangement or hit a wrong note during rehearsals. There were however compensations: later in her career when she was commanding huge fees, she would pay The Echoes more for one performance than they would have earned in a week working for anyone else.

In December 1963, Dusty broke off her tour to travel to Paris. Marlene Dietrich, who not so long ago had disapproved of her "ruining" "Sag mir wo die Blumen sind", had read of her obsession with Burt Bacharach's music, and invited her to her premiere at the Olympia, then as now the most prestigious music-hall in France, if not the whole of Europe. Edith Piaf should have been topping the bill: she had died in October, plunging the whole country into mourning. The theatre's director, Bruno Coquatrix, had brought in Marlene, Piaf's best friend, well aware that its famously tetchy audiences would never settle for second best. In these days, Marlene never worked anywhere without Bacharach. Three months earlier, she had performed his and Hal David's "Anyone Who Had A Heart in one of her recitals—the only time she ever sang it—before handing it over to Bacharach's "star pupil", Dionne Warwick, whose version would sell a million copies by the end of the year. There would follow several cover versions of the song—the most celebrated by Cilla Black, the best by Dusty. Marlene had called Warwick, "The natural successor to Joséphine Baker, a beautiful black pearl," telling me afterwards, "Well, I had to say *something* good about her to keep Bacharach on side!" To placate him, terrified that the pop songs would take over, leaving her to look for a new orchestra leader (which is what eventually happened), she had requested that Warwick be her *vedette-américaine* at the Olympia—this was the artiste, secondary to the top of the bill, who closed the first half of the programme. This had not been possible: the mime-artiste, Marcel Marceau, had been engaged at the same time as Piaf. Warwick was therefore relegated to performing three songs. Preceding her on the bill was 12-year-old Motown prodigy Little Stevie Wonder, who received a lukewarm reception from the audience.

After the show, Dusty met Marlene. "I'd heard her singing on the radio, naturally," she told me some years later, "But until then I'd assmumed she was black. She had that sort of voice, and over the years it got better. When Dusty Springfield sang 'Ne me quitte pas', it broke your heart." It was Marlene who introduced Dusty to Burt Bacharach—who promised to write her a song "very, very soon".

Dusty's three-day trip to Paris enabled her to complete her transformation from "clumsy, red-headed frump" to svelt, sophisticated chanteuse. An avid reader of anything from *Vogue* magazine to the classics, she stopped off at a pavement newspaper kiosk and bought every pop/fashion/women's magazine they had. Their covers were graced with the likes of singers Sylvie Vartan, who she had met in London, Juliette Gréco, the darling of the Existentialists whom she met now—and actresses Catherine Deneuve and Delphine Seyrig. She went to see Seyrig's most celebrated film, *Last Year At Marienbad*, and was soon emulating her slinky stance. Vartan, who also later peroxided her hair, she was keen on at the time, and she commissioned a bobbed, dark-blonde Vartan wig. In 1966, however, she would revise her opinion about the singer when, during the taping of a French pop programme a bunch of Vartan fans who believed her to be imitating their idol began whistling and flicking coins on to the stage—in France in those days, a sign of derision. Dusty also had made a lighter-coloured, slightly more bouffant wig which she would wear with a black velvet band, a la Deneuve. Gréco inspired Dusty's choice in heavy mascara and clothes—tight-fitting, ankle-length "hobble" gowns which she commissioned on pastel colours—Gréco, then as now, strictly adhered to the *chanteuse-réaliste* tradition of only ever wearing black on stage.

Meanwhile, it was back to touring, promotions, and the final preparations for her debut album. Dusty had recently moved into a flat in London's Baker Street—*Ready, Steady, Go!*'s Vicki Wickham lived in the same building. Vic Billing's and Pat Rhodes' major problem was ensuring that she got to each venue on time. She had just bought herself a sports car, and insisted on driving herself to the engagement if this was less than fifty miles from home—otherwise the tour bus would be kept waiting for hours until her team had got her out of bed and "in working order". Though no great party animal, Dusty liked to entertain and often would not get to bed until 4 am, whilst the tour bus usually left its garage near Marylbone Station at eight in the dot. Tempers were therefore often frayed by the time the show hit the road.

On 1 January 1964, the BBC broadcast its very first edition of *Top Of The Pops* from its Manchester Rusholm Studios. Introduced by Jimmy Saville, and with all the artistes miming to their records, Dusty appeared after The Rolling Stones. Also in the line-up were The Dave Clark Five, The Hollies, The Swinging Blue Jeans, and The Beatles who were currently Number One. Even faking it, so to speak, Dusty proved herself a cut above the rest. She also wore so much kohl and mascara that her eyes looked invisible—bringing the quip from Liverpudlian comic Jimmy Tarbuck, "Dusty Springfield went to London Zoo the other day, and Chi-Chi the panda kept winking at her!" There were also more appearances on *Ready, Steady, Go!*, and in February participation in a charity show at the Royal Albert Hall when The Rolling Stones topped the bill. Oddly, Vic Billings was knocked back when he suggested that Dusty should appear on *Sunday Night At The London Palladium*—Val Parnell booked The Beverley Sisters instead, and she threw a fit when she watched them audaciously closing the show with "I Only Want To Be With You".

In the February, Dusty released her second single, "Stay Awhile", which peaked at Number 13 in the charts. She had wanted to release a cover of Bacharach and David's "Anyone Who Had A Heart", which Dionne Warwick had sung at the Olympia, whilst Johnny Franz had been in favour of her recording Gene Pitney's "Twenty-Four Hours From Tulsa". Dusty had reservations about the first song: Warwick had performed it so well, she said, far better than she ever could. Nonsense, of course! Yet she would be mortified when Cilla Black took "her" song to the top of the British charts! Dusty would also befriend Warwick—or at least pretend to—when the

American singer flew to London to promote "Walk On By" later in the year. The two would be snapped drinking pints of beer and enjoying a "chinwag" in an East End pub, and shopping in Carnaby Street and Petticoat Lane Market. It was all for show, to keep Burt Bacharach on side in the hope that he would write her the hit song he had promised. Truthfully, Dusty could not stand Warwick, and Warwick would never forgive her, or Cilla, for stealing "Anyone Who Had A Heart". The fact that both women sang the song far, far better than her was apparenly immaterial. "Tulsa", on the other hand, was she said a great number but would give the fans the wrong impression of her. Would a shy, demure, decent young woman pick up a stranger outside a hotel entrance, as the song suggests, and spend the night with him? It might have been argued that Pitney might not have gone in for casual sex either, if appearances were anything to go by—quite simply because he was so neurotic, and gave on the impression that once he got the girl back to his room, he might be too *frightened* to do anything with her!

The new single attracted fewer promotional appearances than its predecessor: therefore Dusty and Vic Billings flew to New York, where the first item on the agenda was a meeting with Burt Bacharach. She had included three of his songs on her debut album, scheduled for a Spring release, and Bacharach had kept his promise and written a song especially for her. What this was, she never got around to asking: whilst they were dining in his apartment, Bacharach's secretary kept replenishing the turntable, and one of the songs was Bacharach and David's "I Just Don't Know What To Do With Myself", the flipside of Tommy Hunt's 1962 hit, "And I Never Knew". Dusty was bowled over, and announced that she would have this one instead and that it would be her next single after "Stay Awhile". Before leaving New York, she dropped in at the Mira Sound Studios, where she spent much of the day with Shelby Singleton, with whom she had worked on The Springfields' *Folk Songs From The Hills*. Singleton introduced her to Nashville arranger Jerry Kennedy, and the jamming session which ensued would provide her with extra material for her album.

Returning to the UK, Dusty hit the tour trail once more, sharing the bill with Eden Kane. The tabloid gossip-mongers suddenly went into overdrive. Kane's career was on the slide, and it was suggested that Dusty was being paid by his record company to help keep his name in lights until his contract expired. This led to the pair becoming linked romanically, a fabrication which Dusty was happy not to deny because, even this early in her career and despite her intense discretion, she was terrified of losing all that she had worked for by being outed. Speculation about her sexuality was temporarily diffused when she told a *Daily Mirror* reporter, "Yes, I've taken him home to meet my parents." The fact that Kane (aka Richard Sarstedt) may have been Jewish, and that the O'Brien's were devout Catholics was not mentioned. Neither, apparently, was he her only suitor. If one is to believe the hogwash circulating at the time, Dusty was "involved" with four other men: one was supposedly The Echoes' Douggie Reece, two others were gay, and the fourth was the happily married (and also Jewish) Burt Bacharach. A fifth contender, Gene Pitney, was added to this list in the March when Dusty embarked on a three-weeks tour of Australasia with him, Gerry & The Pacemakers, and Brian Poole & The Tremeloes. The ensemble were mobbed by 5,000 fans at Sydney Airport, and similar hysteria awaited them in Melbourne, Adelaide and Wellington. In fact, Dusty did not particularly like the man who brought on-stage neurasthenia to a whole new level. And yet it was he who had the audacity to call *her* a bag of nerves!

From Australia, Dusty flew to Hawaii—for a five-day break without engagements, her first true holiday in years. Then it was back to Britain, where *A Girl Called Dusty* hit the shops in April 1964: it lost little time getting into the charts, peaking at Number Six and staying in the bestsellers list for six months. With a denim-clad Dusty on the cover, this contained an excellent cross-section of ballads, R & B, and Motown covers all of them vastly superior to the originals, it was geared towards the Mods on the dancefloor, with half of the tracks fading accordingly. There is Lesley Gore's "You Don't Own Me", promoted at the time by Gore as a "proto-feminist anthem", Dionne Warwick's "Wishin' & Hopin'", and an upbeat version of Marlene Dietrich's "Shh, kleines Baby"—here Dusty sings the Charlie and Inez Foxx adaptation, "Mockingbird", and duets with herself. There is her own arrangement of The Supremes' "When The Lovelight Starts Shining Through His Eyes", and a so-so cover of Lee Dorsey's hammy "Do Re Mi". Without undue effort, Dusty makes two Shirelles songs her own: "Mama Said", and "Will You Still Love Me Tomorrow?" Next comes Ray Charles' "Don't You Know?"—one of the numbers The Echoes were asked to play for their audition. And finally, the ballads. "Anyone Who Had A Heart" and "Twenty-Four Hours From Tulsa" may be the best songs on the album, but John Kander and Fred Ebb's "My Colouring Book" comes a very close third. This had been written for Barbra Streisand in 1962, though Nana Mouskouri had recorded it at the same time and sold more copies.

In May, Dusty flew to Italy, where she spent a week sightseeing in Rome, Naples—and Capri, where she lunched with Gracie Fields at her Canzone del Mare complex, and attended a Luigi Tenco concert. Tenco (1939-67) had a deep, smoky voice and sounded a little like Nat King Cole. He specialised in passionate, heartfelt ballads, and Dusty was taken up by his "Mi sono innamorato di te", which he gave her permission to have adapted into English. Dusty was desperate to give Cilla Black and Sandie Shaw a run for their money by proving that they did not hold the monopoly on high-powered ballads. Both had recently hit the jackpot with Bacharach-David songs—Sandie with "Always Something There To Remind Me", Cilla with "Anyone Who Had A Heart" and more recently with "You're My World, introduced by Tenco's contemporary, Umberto Bindi, another song which Dusty had had her eye on for a while. Now, she called Vic Billings from Rome, told him about the Tenco song, and demanded that "I Just Don't Know What To Do With Myself" be withdrawn. It was too late in the day to do this, and the record was released without her blessing. It acually sold more copies than "You're My World"—only The Beatles' "A Hard Day's Night" and The Rolling Stones' "It's All Over Now" prevented it from topping the charts. The song was undoubedly Dusty's best so far, though some critics—and even a few fans— would poke fun at her extraneous gestures while performing it. One wag suggested that the reason she flung her arms up to her face while belting out these powerhouse numbers was because the emotion sometimes got to be too much for her and she forgot the words, therefore she printed these on her wrists! In fact, she was so short-sighted that, even if she had done this, on a darkened stage it would have been impossible to see them. Additionally, the audience would have seen them when the house lights came on. Dusty was not exaggerating when she said that, much of the time, she could not see the television cameras even when these were only yards in front of her—a problem which she solved by having the cameraman attach a piece of white card to the tripod. The song, moreso than Cilla's early successes, also set a valuable precedent in that it introduced to Britain a new genre of anguished up-tempo love songs previously championed by Continental stars such as Gribouille ("Mathias") and Francoise Hardy ("All Over The World"). Other British girl singers would attempt this very specialised medium: Dusty, Cilla, Marianne and Sandie aside, most would be one-hit wonders.

Scarcely pausing to catch her breath when she returned home, Dusty hopped back on to her tour bus and, after spending six weeks zigzagging up and down the country, began what should have been a week-long stint in Coventry with The Searchers and Eden Kane. After the fifth show she was forced to bow out through laryngitis. While she was recuperating, Vic Billings was contacted by the organisers of Murray The K's Extravaganza, a twice-nightly showcase at New York's multiracial 5,000-seater Fox Theater, in Brooklyn, after the Apollo in Harlem the most important venue for the city's black community.

Between 1958-9, Murray Kaufman (1922-82) virtually ruled the New York air waves. Single-handedly, this extraordinary man integrated black, white and Latino performers on the same stage, long before the US government passed its civil rights laws. More importantly, he did so without causing any fuss amongst distractors—once joking that the only ever riots he had incurred had been those en-route to the box-office. Bobby Darin and Dionne Warwick got their big breaks through him, as did Martha Reeves of The Vandellas. Always introduced with a Frank Sinatra song, Kaufman's shows would be broadcast from just about anywhere to attract maximum publicity: subways, fighter jets, baseball stadiums—one, in a New York square during a snowstorm with bikini-clad cheerleaders! A self-confessed megalomaniac and six times married, Kaufman also raised hundreds of thousands of dollars for refugees.

During the early years of Beatlemania, Murray Kaufman was known as The Fifth Beatle—an appellation said to have come from George Harrison. He had been the first American DJ to be accepted into the group's inner circle, whence he had developed a mania for absolutely anything Liverpudlian. When his aides had suggested bringing a white singer over from England to perform black songs at the Fox Theater, Kaufman had balked at the idea—his argument being that *only* black singers were capable of singing black music properly. When he heard "You're My World" on the radio and was erroneously told that this was Liverpool's most famous singer, Dusty Springfield, he changed his mind. It was only when Dusty arrived in New York, accompanied by her parents, that Kaufman realised she was not Cilla! His producer wanted to send her packing, but once they had auditioned her in the empty theatre and heard how good she was, they upped her fee for the twenty shows!

Dusty later said that her tenure at the Fox had been like a trip to heaven, for here she was sharing equal billing with names she had only ever dreamed of meeting: Martha & The Vandellas, Marvin Gaye, The Temptations—and The Ronettes, whose dressing room she was asked to share. Also present were Phil and Ronnie Spector, whilst human rights activist Malcom X dropped in each day for a chat. Because of his presence and the tension this caused outside the theatre, once the singers arrived for the morning rehearsal they were not permitted to leave the building until after the show, twelve hours later. Dusty, star-struck from the moment she met these people— though she was just as big in her field as they were in theirs— recalled in an interview with Radio One,

> It was a dream come true. It was priceless. I would have paid to do it. I was the token whitey, the token honkey....I blundered my way through Harlem not knowing what was around me, a beehive surrounded by pimps, hookers, addicts and pushers. I stayed at the Hotel Teresa, with broken windows. Malcolm X was there. God protects fools and innocents. I grew up fast!

What Dusty did not add was that her first working experience with her R & B idols started off as a nighmare. Upon her arrival in New York there had been no welcoming committee and she had had to make her own way to the theatre, where one of Murray Kaufman's assistants had showed her to her dressing room and rudely left her to introduce herself to everyone else. Though she would only be singing two songs in each show ("Wishin' & Hopin'", and "I Only Want To Be With You"), there would be as many as six shows a day, leaving little time for socialising between performances. Kaufman had appointed Martha & The Vandellas as her backing group, and as part of the team effort Dusty would also be expected to back the other singers from the wings. Meeting Dusty came as a big shock to these people. All of them had heard her on the radio, but few knew what she looked like, and the first thing that hit them was that she was not black. Not that anyone was in any way prejudiced or unfriendly towards her—quite the reverse, they were proud that an attractive white woman had taken it upon herself to champion their style. What they did not anticipate was her unpredictable temper. Her nerves frayed over the fact that she

she might fail and make a fool of herself, she yelled and cursed whenever she hit a sour note and took a leaf out of her mother's book by flinging whatever crockery was at hand at the walls. Far from criticising her and complaining to the producer, the other artistes simply regarded her as "the eccentric English girl", and eventually found amusement in her tantrums because they were mostly directed at herself. Martha Reeves would go on to become a close friend—they even put in an impromptu performance at the Apollo, at a time when white artistes just did not appear there—and the other singers adopted Dusty as their lucky mascot on account of her being the only white person on the Fox Theater bill. On a more serious note she began drinking, though not too heavily for now—one of The Temptations is said to have handed her a tumbler of vodka to help calm her nerves, with Dusty apparently so liking the taste that she finished off the bottle.

Immediately after the Kaufman shows, Dusty embarked on what should have been an eight-date tour of America with Eden Kane and The Searchers. Halfway through this, in Tulsa, thirty minutes before the show she collapsed from nervous exhaustion—hardly surprising after being cooped in the Fox Theater for ten, twelve-hour days without seeing daylight. Neither had she seen much of her parents, who had been joined by Tom and escorted around New York, finally flying home without saying goodbye. The doctor who examined her prescribed complete rest, but Dusty insisted on performing: she managed ten songs before leaving the stage. The next day, rather than take her home, Vic Billings booked her on a flight to the Caribbean, where she spent ten days relaxing in the sun.

Fully recovered, Dusty returned to England where, on 16 October, her fourth single was released: penned by brother Tom and Clive Westlake, "Losing You" (backed with Tom Springfield and Clive Westlake's Top 30 hit for Frank Ifield, "Summer Is Over") peaked at Number 9 in the charts. Later in the month, she acted as Martha & The Vandella's ambassador when the group arrived in London. She and the trio appeared on *Ready, Steady, Go!*, and Dusty took her new friend shopping and sightseeing.

Mary Wells had paved the way for Motown artistes in Britain by getting "My Guy" into the Top Five, and soon she would be followed across the Atlantic by The Supremes and several other big acts, all of which would be taken under Dusty's wing. There followed a brief tour with Dave Berry, Herman's Hermits, and Brian Poole & The Tremeloes. Each evening, Dusty opened her set with "Dancing In The Street", and managed to get in two songs she said she wished she had introduced—Doris Day's "Secret Love" from *Calamity Jane* (also a recent hit for Kathy Kirby) and Sandie Shaw's "Always Something There To Remind Me". She should have appeared in the *Royal Variety Performance* on 8 November, but was replaced at the last minute by Cilla Black—which did not bode well with her at all. In early December she released a Christmas single, "O Holy Child", another song penned by Tom. The record did not chart, though all the royalties went to Dr Bernardo's Homes for disabled children.

In the middle of December, Dusty and her musicians flew to South Africa for what should have been a seven-date tour of the townships surrounding Capetown, Johannesburg and Port Elizabeth. Vic Billings had flown on ahead of her, hoping to smooth the way in what was expected to be a volatile climate regarding the country's stance on apartheid. Some years before, George and Beryl Formby had been performing to a segregated audience when a little black girl had walked on to the stage to present them with flowers. Beryl had picked her up, kissed her, and the next day the couple had been asked to leave the country. Instead, they had defied the authorities by performing in the townships to blacks only audiences. They had got away with this because, according to a loophole in the law, segregation did not apply if the venue was a cinema which seated less than 1,500 people, though they had eventually been deported. Diana Dors had experienced similar problems during a cabaret tour, and the result had been the same when she had refused to present a sporting award at an event where black sportsmen had been excluded.

Dusty would not prove quite so daring. "I've got a special clause written into the contract which stipulates that I shall only play to non-segregated audiences. That's my little bit to help coloured people there," she told the *New Musical Express,* adding that if the South African authorities tried to force her to do otherwise, she would be on the first place home. Billings had been told that performing to mixed audiences was against the law and would not be tolerated, even though some theatres allowed this—he does not, however, appear to have made this very clear to Dusty, though in his defence he had booked Dusty *only* in those cinemas where the Formbys and Diana Dors had played, all those years ago. Dusty would be taken to task for not walking off the stage upon seeing the mixed rows of black and white faces. In fact, like George Formby, she was so short-sighted that she could barely see the footlights, let alone who was sitting in the stalls.

When faced with angry officials, Beryl Formby had given as good as she got—even slapping the South African prime minister across the face. Dusty simply mumbled an apology, and promptly burst into tears. Vic Billings covered his own back by declaring that he had explained the regulations to his client, but that she had refused to listen. The fact that Dusty had already publicly declared that she would be donating her entire earnings from this tour—estimated at around £3,000—to orphaned *black* children was also added to her list of "crimes". The first two shows in Johannesburg went without hitch—just a handful of racist protesters outside the venue. So too did things appear to be running smoothly during the first shows at the Luxurama Theatre, in Wittebome, an establishment with a no-refunds policy. The authorities had been watching her, however, and on the eve of her fifth of seven concerts she was ordered not to sing in front of a mixed audience—for a non-segregated show which had sold out weeks ago. Not wishing to let these fans down, Dusty did the show. The manager, a Mr Quibbell, presented her with flowers after the performance, kissed her on both cheeks—then hypocritically alerted the military police to complain that she had "broken the house rules" by boasting her ability "to bring blacks and whites together in harmony". Two hours later, three government officials barged into her hotel suite and served her with a pledge: unless she signed this, swearing not to play before mixed audiences, she would be compelled to leave the country within the next twenty-four hours.

Dusty's refusal to comply resulted in her passport being impounded, and the phone in her room cut off so that she could not make contract with the outside world. She was served with a deportation order and transferred to a hotel in Johannesburg, where she was informed that two seats had been reserved on a flight for London the next day—one for her, the other for Vic Billings. She refused to leave the country without The Echoes, who were staying in another hotel in the city, having only just been made aware of what was happening. After ploughing through a mountain of red tape, Billings managed to secure everyone seats on the same plane, and early the next evening Dusty and The Echoes were collected from their respective hotels and escorted to the airport by an armed guard. Unable to mix with the other passengers in the departure lounge, they were marched across the tarmac to the waiting plane, where a line of black porters doffed their caps out of respect. Dusty's response, however, to the white official who saluted as she mounted the steps was a pronounced, "Fuck you!"

The South African government issued a brief statement: "Miss Springfield received two warning regarding her flounting of this country's entertainments laws, and twice she refused to comply. She broke the law, and as such has paid the penalty. From today her records will be banned in South Africa." The British government, recognising this, refused to intervene. At Heathrow, Dusty received a heroine's welcome, cheered by more than a thousand fans. Purposely choosing a black and white chair, she told the barrage of press, "I may sue the South African government. If they want to sling mud around, they've picked the wrong person because I have a far more deadly aim." And, she was asked, would she go back if she had the chance? "Sure," she replied, "The audiences were fantastic and the kids were marvellous. But I won't be going back until they sort this thing out, which I don't think will be in my lifetime."

The debacle would continue for several months. Comedian Max Bygraves, one-hit wonders Peter & Gordon, and snooty character actor Derek Nimmo, about to begin working in South Africa, accused Dusty of aggravating the political situation there by organising a publicity stunt and effectively making conditions intolerable there for people like themselves. Dusty responded by calling Nimmo "a pompous prat"—what she had to say about the others may not be repeated here. "I have no political views," she hit back in an interview which, tragically, did not receive a wider audience because it was given to *Melody Maker* and not the national press, "But if anyone pays me the compliment of wanting to watch me on the stage, then they should be allowed to buy a ticket irrespective of colour, creed or religion." On the positive side, on 19 December a small governmental group headed by fifteen MPs pledged a motion to make a public stand against "the obnoxious doctrine of apartheid in South Africa". Shortly after this, the United Nations Special Committee Against Apartheid, aided by singer Miriam Makeba and trumpeter Hugh Masekela, petitioned for an international cultural boycott against South Africa. This helped somewhat—The Searchers, The Zombies, and Eden Kane all cancelled their imminent trips to the country—but as Dusty had forecast, it would take years for this disease to be stamped out altogether.

Chapter Four

Don't Let Me Lose This Dream

T he new year dawned with Dusty making a double appearance at the famed San Remo Festival, in Italy. Paired with Fabrizio Ferretti (as per the contest's tradition) she sang "Tu che ne sai" and was eliminated in the first round. Her second song, "Di fronte all'amore", which saw her paired with Gianni Mascolo, made it through to the semi-finals—she would later record this in English as "I Will Always Want You". Dusty celebrated her loss by rushing to her room and decimating an expensive vase. Two years later, Dalida and her lover Luigi Tenco would share this same room and come second in the contest with "Ciao, amore, ciao", and the outcome would be even more dire: accusing officials of rigging the voting, he would take a revolver and blow his brains out. The overall winner in 1965 was Bobby Solo & The New Christy Minstrels, with "Se piang, se ridi". Dusty thought about having this adapted into English, but instead plumped for the song which came seventh—Pino Donaggio's "Io che non vivo", of which more later.

In the February, Dusty released Mike Hawker and Ivor Raymonde's "Your Hurtin' Kinda Love", a dramatic piece which received the thumbs-down from fans, barely scraping into the

Top 40. She sang this on *Sunday Night At The London Palladium* before jetting off to New York: "I Only Want To Be With You" had entered the *Billboard* chart, where it would peak at Number 12. Then it was off to Rio, where she spent five days at the Carnival with Martha Reeves and Madeline Bell, a sojourn which ended when she stepped on a broken bottle, badly gashing her foot. Returning to Britain and in obvious pain, she embarked on the three-weeks tour with The Searchers. 1964 had seen readers of the *New Musical Express* voting her Top British Female Vocalist, and second only to Brenda Lee in the World category. This led to her performing a set at the magazine's Poll Winners Concert, at Wembley's Empire Pool.

Soon afterwards, Dusty hosted her first television show, a one-hour *Ready, Steady, Go!* special entitled *Dusty Springfield Presents The Sound Of Motown*—a title which, prior to its broadcast on 28 April had been whittled down to *The Sound Of Motown*. It coincided with the label's launch in Britain, for which Berry Gordy had assembled a tour with Stevie Wonder, The Supremes, The Miracles, and of course Martha & The Vandellas—the latter's high-charged duet with Dusty of "Wishin' & Hopin'" was the hilight of the television show. When filming wrapped, a huge Motown party took place in Holland Park where guests of honour were Dusty, The Rolling Stones' Brian Jones, Sandie Shaw, The Seekers and The Animals. The actual tour kicked off on 30 April will a sell-out show at Finsbury Park, though without celebrity support at the subsequent venues would be lucky if they played to 50 per cent capacity audiences. Then for Dusty it was back to the old routine—a Northern clubland tour which coincided with the release of a new single, "In The Middle Of Nowhere", a rowdy but infectious piece which featured Madeleine Bell and another Springfield regular, ex-gospel singer Doris Troy, on backing vocals, with The Animal's Alan Price on piano. Unlike its predecessor it had no trouble getting into the Top Ten. Later, Dusty's "choir" would be augmented by Lesley Duncan and British newcomer Kiki Dee, and under the pseudonym Gladys Thong (to get around the clause in her contract prohibiting her from doing so) Dusty returned the compliment by singing backing vocals on some of their records.

At around this time, Dusty moved home, renting a flat within a large regency house on Westbourne Terrace, near Hyde Park. The other occupants included Margo Lewis and Carole MacDonald of Goldie & The Gingerbreads, "Little Arrows" singer Leapy Lee, woman DJ Stevie Holly, and Madeleine Bell. Vicki Wickham spent so much time here that she almost considered herself a resident. Another frequent visitor was Lee Everett, wife of outrageous DJ Kenny. Then there were Dusty's tennis friends, chief of which were Billie Jean King and Rosie Casals. Some of the food-throwing parties here were legendary, especially when the O'Briens came to stay, or if everyone had been smoking pot. Her tenancy here would be brief. Soon afterwards she would move to a three-storey house on Aubrey Walk, which she would share with "Walking My Cat Named Dog" singer Norma Tanega. The pair had been friends for a while since appearing on television's *Thank Your Lucky Stars*, with the press speculating over whether they were actually lovers. They were, but though Dusty was absolutely terrified of anyone ever finding out, Tanega said she would have loved to have been as outrageous as Madonna, and held nothing back. In those days, of course, homophobia was rife in the music industry and such an admission would not have been tolerated.

Dusty should have played a short summer season in Bournemouth, but this was cancelled when she was admitted to a London clinic suffering from acute nervous exhaustion. Her problem had always been worrying for worrying's sake, searching for problems which were not there, then getting worked up over nothing. Like her former idols Peggy Lee and Doris Day, she was a perfectionist: unlike them, she was incapable of handling fame and appears to have been anything but relaxed much of the time, especially while working in the studio. When it came to musical arrangements, Dusty knew exactly what she wanted and would never settle for second best, flying off the handle with her musicians over the slightest discrepancy. Also, as her career progressed, she became increasingly more paranoid about her appearance. As had happened with some of the stars from the old studio system—Garbo, Dietrich, Crawford—virtually no one was permitted to see her not looking her absolute best. Much as she loved being recognised, despite the frequently flimsy disguise of headscarf and dark glasses, she loathed being photographed unless for an authentic shoot. Like Garbo, if a press photographer approached unexpectedly, she would shield her face with whatever was closest at hand. More often than not, preparation for the performance took longer than the performance itself, and involved tremendous peronal discomfort. East End drag-queens, who had formerly championed Dorothy Squires and Marlene Dietrich, now had a new alter-ego. On planes, so as not to disturb her heavily lacquered wigs, Dusty would sleep for hours sitting bolt upright. The make-up, particularly the mascara, often looked like it had been applied with a trowel to the extent that, at times, she appeared not to have any eyes. Sometimes she would begin fixing this on the plane, not get it finished before the plane landed, then stumble through the airport late at night so that no one would see her "naked" eyes. She had created this mythical image. Mary O'Brien was dead and buried. The wigs became more elaborate, and were named after rivals—Cilla, Sandie, Lulu, etc. Therefore if one of these singers upset her by "pinching" one of her songs, or if she was just generally in a bad mood, she could fling the hairpiece across the room or trample it underfoot. The music journalist Keith Altham recalled dropping in at the *Ready, Steady, Go!* studio to find her throwing one of her wigs around: "I said, 'Hi, Dusty. Am I interrupting something?' She said, 'I'm just giving Cilla a good kicking!'"

Dusty was also paranoid about her off-stage privacy. Friends recall her dashing into the bathroom if room service knocked on the door, or into the next room if the window cleaner came around. She was also terrified of forgetting the words to her songs and a bag of nerves before going on stage, convinced that she would mess up and end up with audiences laughing or walking out on her. This never happened. Though she would give some pretty mediocre performances towards the end of her life on account of her final illness, the fans always stuck by her and if she did slip up, they would prompt her by singing along. Yet if she did make a mistake, Dusty would don the proverbial hair-shirt and feel bad for days. Her only "cure" would come with flinging food at the walls, turning her flat or dressing room into a pig-sty. Then, she would engage in what she called her therapeutic passion—cleaning. Like Joan Crawford, she loved nothing better than getting down on her hands and knees, preferably in an expensive gown, and fettling the place from top to bottom. Shopping was another way of relieving the tension, though as a shopaholic she had been tempered somewhat in the habit by Vic Billings, who at around this time began investing/banking her earnings, said to have been in excess of £2,000 a week, and paying her a weekly allowance.

In September 1965, following an extended holiday in the Virgin Islands, Dusty released a new single, "Some Of Your Lovin'", a heady ballad penned by Gerry Goffin and Carole King, which reached Number 8 in the charts. Simultaneously she released her second album, *Everything's Coming Up Dusty*. Philips spared no expense with the packing: an attractive gatefold sleeve containing a 12-page photo spread mostly of stills from her television appearances, unusual for the time. Technically, this album was better than *A Girl Called Dusty*—less fade-outs, for one thing—though despite peaking at Number 6 in the charts it did not shift as many copies, albeit that it has made up for this since.

The album opens well with the gospel-tinged "Won't Be Long", though with "Oh No! Not My Baby", a recent hit for Manfred Mann, Dusty is almost completely drowned by Madeleine Bell. Next comes Bacharach and David's "Long After Tonight Is Over", originally a hit for Jimmy Radcliffe, another star who would die tragically young. "La Bamba" is a traditional song, revided by Richie Havens in 1958 and a hit across the Continent for Dalida. Singing in Spanish here, Dusty is accompanied on the Latin piano by her brother Tom. She does not however exonerate herself well with Anthony Newley and Leslie Bricusse's showstopper, "Who Can I Turn To?", a minor hit for Tony Bennett which Dionne Warwick had recently murdered. Dusty emulates the Peggy Lee Latin version, which just does not work here. With Ray Charles ' "Doodlin'", something of an upbeat torch song, she fares slightly better. Much better is "If It Don't Work Out", albeit a little heavy on the percussion: this was especially written for Dusty by The Zombies' Rod Argent, who provides piano accompaniment. She wanted this to be released as her next single, but Philips overruled her: in the mid-Sixties, unlike today, it was not customary to release singles taken from albums because record companies were afraid that if this happened, fans would only buy one or the other. Above average are "That's How Heartaches Are Made", and Garnett Mimms' "It Was Easier To Hurt Him", a recent hit for Wayne Fontana. "I've Been Wrong Before" is a simplistic reading of the Randy Newman song most associated with Cilla Black, who sings it better. Madeleine Bell and Doris Troy again share the honours with "I Can't Hear You", "Packin' Up", and "I Had A Talk With Your Man". Dusty had also recorded an excellent version of The Velvettes' "Needle In A Haystack", but this was dropped when, upon listening to the playback tape, she declared that she no longer liked it.

At the end of October, despite being warned by her doctor to take things easy, Dusty flew to New York, then on to Los Angeles where she spent a week doing the rounds of television variety and chat shows. She was back in London for 14 November, for her only appearance on a *Royal Variety Show*. Topping the bill was Shirley Bassey. Dusty wasdisappointed that she was asked to sing just one song—"I Just Don't Know What To Do With Myself"—and that more emphasis was placed on French counterpart, Sylvie Vartan, who with her rocker husband Johnny Hallyday stole the show.

Following an explosive appearance on *Ready, Steady, Go!*'s New Year special which saw her raucously duetting with Lulu ("Let's Hang On"), Dusty released her first single off 1966:

"Little By Little" was written for her by "Middle Of Nowhere" composers Bea Verdi and Buddy Kaye. Another gospel-styled anthem backed by regulars Madeleine Bell, Lesley Duncan and Kiki Dee, it sneaked into the Top Twenty, but only after Philips had advertised it in the music press. Dusty confessed to never liking the song, which of course begs the question—why bother recording it in the first place?

Nothing would ever compare with Dusty's next single. Philips had wanted this to be "Heartbeat"—not the Buddy Holly hit and later theme of the television drama series, but the Gloria Jones number which the company planned releasing simultaneously in America. Dusty stuck to her guns: she had never been satisfied with their choice of releases there, and from now on declared that nothing would be issued without her approval. Also, though she did not actually dislike Cilla Black, she was irked with the fact that Cilla was selling more records in the UK than herself—for no other reason than Cilla specialised in powerhouse Continental ballads which she seemed to have been born to sing. Dusty therefore decided that her next single on *both* sides of the Atlantic would be an English adaptation of "Io che non vivo", which Pino Donaggio and songwriter partner Vito Pallavicini had given her permission to use—on the proviso that their arrangement remain unchanged. Dusty had attempted to write the lyrics herself, as had Tom, adhering as close as possible to the song's original meaning, "I can't live without you". This had not worked and, according to the story, hoping that someone would come up with a solution to her dilemma, Dusty instructed Johnny Franz to book the studio, then asked her friend Vicki Wickham to "sort it". Wickham later claimed to have met pop guru Simon Napier Bell that same evening and that between them they had written the lyrics in a matter of hours, which may or may not be true. What *is* important is that they came up with arguably the most important song of Dusty's career.

"You Don't Have To Say You Love Me", recorded (Take 53 of 59) in a stairwell to get the acoustics spot on, is the kind of *symphonie-en-miniature* which would have done Squires or

Garland proud: the stirring horn introduction, the subtle but complicated key-changes, the way the music builds up to a stunning crescendo, the intense but simplistic, passionate, heart-on-sleeve lyrics which have far more sincerity than the original Italian ones. Released in March 1966, it shot to the top of the British charts, giving Dusty her only Number One here, and though it only held the top spot for one week, it provided her flagging confidence with a much needed boost. In America it peaked at Number 4, and proved so popular that the *Everything's Coming Up Dusty* album was retitled to accommodate this as the title-track. Of the many cover versions, arguably the most famous was by Elvis Presley, who recorded it in 1970. With this song, Dusty's very own *hymne a l'amour* which shifted a million copies by the end of the year, she had moved as far from her Motown roots as was possible whilst well aware of the risks she was taking. This was reflected in the mixed public reaction towards it, not helped by her own statement that she believed Pino Donaggio's to have been the superior version of the song. Television's *Juke Box Jury* even voted it a "miss". Some tabloid journalists wanted to know who the love interest in the song was supposed to be—whether this was a he or a she. In fact, the unnamed recipient of Dusty's affection could just as easily have been her thousands of fans as opposed to one person in particular. At the time of writing, in its many versions Donaggio's song had sold a staggering 80 million records worldwide, but few would argue that it will never truly belong to anyone but Dusty Springfield.

In the summer of 1966, Dusty was signed for her first six-part television series, simply titled *Dusty*. The first show went out on 18 August: the 30-piece orchestra was conducted by Johnny Pearson, whilst Madeleine Bell, Lesley Duncan and The Ladybirds provided backing vocals. Her fabulous gowns were designed by Rita Reekie and Dusty's couturier friend, Eric Darnell (who also designed for Diana Dors), created in her favourite shades of pink and purple, and frequently complimented by flowers in her hair or pinned to her neckline—

not that this mattered much to anyone but her because everything was filmed in monochrome. The producer wanted these to be alternated—short, flouncy dresses for the pop and Motown numbers, ankle-length gowns for the ballads, but Dusty refused to compromise. Her "foible" would presently apply to the recording studio, invariably resulting in her delaying the proceedings in that it took her almost as long to decide on which dress to wear as it did for her to apply her make-up. "She thought her legs were less than lovely," *Dusty In Memphis* producer Jerry Wexler recalled, "And when she finally arrived, she would be swathed in fabric to the floor."

Petula Clark and Cilla Black had incorporated comedy sketches into their shows, but with Dusty only the music mattered—five songs usually, with a guest spot slotted in the middle—and the series presented her with the opportunity to showcase all those songs she had wanted to record, but never got around to doing so. The first show saw her performing material as diverseThe Four Tops' "Something About You" and The Seekers' "The Olive Tree" before duetting with The Dudley Moore Trio on "Dat Dere". In the second she sang "Cockeyed Optimist", raised the roof with The Isley Brothers' "Take Me In Your Arms", and rounded off the proceedings with "I Just Don't Know What To Do With Myself". Show three included "Twenty-Four Hours From Tulsa" and Paul Francis Webster's "The Mood I'm In": the special guest was Woody Allen. She opened the fourth jazz-themed show with "Call Me Irresponsible", duetted with The Four Freshman, and followed this with a stunning interpretation of Doris Day's "I'll Never Stop Loving You" from the Ruth Etting biopic, *Love Me Or Leave Me*. Her key changes in this difficult song are quite extraordinary. Fans were kept waiting until show five for "You Don't Have To Say You Love Me". In the final show she sang Mary Wells' "You Lost The Sweetest Boy"—and "Anna", in "cod" Spanish, accompanying herself on the guitar and emulating the way Peggy Lee had performed songs such as "Manana". Finally, there was the Jimmy Van Heusen-Sammy Cahn standard, "To Love And Be Loved".

"You Don't Have To Say You Love Me" was still in the lower reaches of the charts when the series aired, and its successor, Gerry Goffin and Carole King's "Goin' Back" had just entered the Top Ten. With its plaintive piano introduction and powerfully undulating strings, the lyrics of this wistful pastiche are deceptively simple but emotive, expressing the narrator's yearning to return to those innocent childhood days the singer claimed to have loved so much. To add to the ambiance, Dusty took her mascot, a moth-eaten teddy bear named Einstein, into the booth when she recorded it. There had been competition in the form of an inferior version by Dusty's friends, Goldie & The Gingerbreads, but their single had been enforcibly withdrawn after they had changed the lyrics without acquiring the composers' permission. Two years later, The Byrds would include it on their *Notorious Byrd Brothers* album. Equally stirring was its successor, "All I See Is You", Clive Westlake's torchy ballad which Dusty released in the September. This reached Number 9 in the UK, Number 20 in America. Philips also put out her first compilation album, *Golden Hits*, which narrowly missed hitting the top spot and remained in the charts for nine months.

In the October, Dusty hit the road, headlining above The Alan Price Set and Dave Berry. Both *Melody Maker* and the *New Musical Express* voted her Top British Female Singer, but whilst she was making headlines in the music press, she also provided fodder for the tabloids. The first was related to her obsession with throwing things. One evening, in a London restaurant, she threw the first thing that came to hand—a meat pie—at a waiter who she thought was being rude to a young female customer. A perfect aim, this hit him at the back of the head. Her "reprehensible" behaviour—compared to the antics of some of today's stars, very tame—was recounted on several front pages, but it was Dusty who had the last word. "I would never dream of throwing a common meat pie at anyone," she told one hack, "It was a quiche lorraine—much more up-market!"

Another more serious incident resulted in a dangerous driving charge. Driving late at night in her sports car and wearing sunglasses to disguise her unmade-up eyes, Dusty hit an old lady crossing Berkeley Square. She was so hysterical after the accident that the paramedics took her to the hospital with the patient. Both she and her unnamed female passenger admitted to the police that it had been her fault entirely, and the matter was turned over to the courts. Unfortunately, the hearing slipped Dusty's mind and when the case was heard at the end of the month she had left England for New York to play a three-week season at Basin Street East. As soon as she realised her gaff, she wired a cheque to the old lady as a down-payment for the damages she knew she would have to pay. In her absence, the judge found her guilty, and awarded the victim £2,000 in damages.

Dusty would not forget Basin Street East in a hurry. The swanky nightclub inside the Sheldon Towers Hotel (now the Shelton Grill) had played host to some of the biggest names in jazz-contemporary music: Peggy Lee had famously played here in 1961. Dusty had been booked for two shows a night, three on weekends, which meant that she would be singing upwards of thirty songs with not much of a break between performances. The supporting act was Buddy Rich (1917-87), the self-professed "world's greatest drummer", and arguably one of the most odious men in American show business. Even his entourage secretly filmed his tantrums and vulgar outbursts and played them back to him, to no avail, in the hope of getting him to clean up his act. In the near future, Rich almost make a second career out of his hatred of The Osmonds, telling one British chat show host in a live programme that his greatest ambition was to "stamp on Little Jimmy Osmond's head". Rich also hated female entertainers, most especially if they were not American, and at Basin Street East aimed his vitriol at Dusty *before* she arrived at the venue— getting his aides to change the sign above the entrance so that his name appeared above hers, and in bigger letters.

Rather than complain, Dusty attempted to suck up to Rich's non-existent better nature—suggesting a jamming session in the hope of persuading his musicians to join her on stage for a couple of numbers. His response, repeated by a blushing Dusty in a *Q* magazine interview shortly after his death, was a spat out, "You fucking broad. Who do you think you fucking are, bitch?" Peggy Lee had faced a similar barrage of insults, and simply walked away. Dorothy Squires has thought about "belting him one". Dusty went the whole hog and rewarded him with a resounding crack across the face, and as she moved away one of her rings caught in his toupee, whipping this off his head and bringing guffaws of laughter from others in the room at the time. "What a bastard," she told *Q*, "He was the arsehole of the world." Rich threatened to sue her for assault, but opted not to do so when she called his bluff and told him to go ahead—there were plenty of witnesses to the incident, and what he had said. Instead, he took to insulting her on stage in front of the audience, who initially believed it to be but part of a comedy repartee, until made wiser by the press. Rich would introduce her with, "She's supposed to be a great singer, but I've heard better."—-or, "She'll be singing 'Sunny', so let's hope that it rains on the broad." His vilest put down was when he said of her, "She's third-rate, just like all those black broads she favours." And Dusty would walk meekly on to the stage and give him two fingers. Some nights, Rich's cronies would come to Basin Street East and encourage him in his despicable behaviour, though Dusty emerged from the situation smelling of roses when other stars turned up supporting her. One was bandleader Benny Goodman, another Peggy Lee— the only time they ever met—who congratulated her on her fine choice of material. Peggy later said that Dusty's interpretation of Billie Holiday's "God Bless The Child" had made her cry. The feud with Rich also ensured that she sang to a packed house every performance. At the end of the run, Rich's musicians— who allegedly only stayed with him because he paid them so well, came back on stage and presented her with a pair of boxing gloves. Attached was the message, "To our champ. You were brave enough to do what we couldn't." Dusty and Rich's paths would cross again in the future, but she would always refuse to acknowledge him.

Towards the end of the year, Dusty found hserself signing up for the time-honoured British tradition of pantomime. She had known the country's top drag artiste, Danny La Rue, for a while. His specialities during the mid-Sixties included celebrity gay icons Marlene Dietrich, Dorothy Squires—and Dusty, who had attended his long-running camp spectacular, *Queen Passionella & The Sleeping Beauty*, the previous year. Meeting producer Tom Arnold after the show, Dusty had joked that it had always been a dream of hers to play pantomime, and in October Arnold called her in New York. He and London's most eminent impresario, Bernard Delfont, wanted her to headline in *Merry King Cole* at the Liverpool Empire. At first she said no: she had just turned down *Dick Whittington*, opposite Eden Kane at the Westcliff Pavillion. Delfont made her an offer she could not refuse—£2,000 a week, along with complete control over her choice of songs for the show. Dusty still hedged, claiming that her fans would never accept her as principal boy—she did not wish to wear a skimpy costume and show her legs, but more crucially she was more worried about the press speculating over her sexuality, should she play a man. Delfont informed her that she would be permitted to wear whatever she wanted, and that her part in the show would be a "mini-recital" towards the end. Furthermore, she would not have to interact with the rest of the cast if she did not want to. Tremulously, she signed the contract and commissioned six floor-length gowns from Eric Darnell.

Merry King Cole opened to rave reviews on 9 January 1967. Dusty got along famously with her co-stars—Blackpool Circus clown Charlie Cairoli, comic Peter Goodwight, and singing twins Paul & Barry Ryan—but she still took Bernard Delfont up on his offer to bill her as "a show within a show". She sang six songs, including both sides of her soon to be released single. "I'll Try Anything" was penned by Mark Barkan, whose "Pretty Flamingo" had taken Manfred Mann to the top of the charts—this one reached Number 13. The B-side, "The Corrupt Ones"—an unusual choice for a pantomime!—was sung by Dusty over the credits of a German espionage film, *Die Holle von Macao*, starring Robert Stack and Elke Sommer. After performing this, she launched herself into the spirit of the pantomime by engaging the audience into a singalong—adopting the snooty mien of an old-fashioned schoolma'am, she stood in front of a large screen and used a large screen to point out the words to "The More I See You" and The Beatles' "Yellow Submarine". Each performance saw her finishing to a standing ovation, but when the run ended she made it very clear that her first pantomine season would also be her last.

On 8 May, Dusty opened at London'sTalk of the Town, the city's premiere cabaret situated at the corner of Charing Cross Road and Leicester Square. Formerly the Hippodrome (to which it would revert in 1982 when purchased by Peter Stringfellow), the venue would host legendary appearances by some of the world's greatest gay icons, including Judy Garland and Eartha Kitt. She was booked here for three weeks, longer than the regular season, for a fee of £3,000 a week, putting her in the same salary bracket as Shirley Bassey, who attended the first night. She was accompanied by the club's resident orchestra, directed by Bert Rhodes, who suggested that she slightly amend her Motown-inspired repertoire to fit in with the posh dining crowd's more sophisticated tastes. For Dusty, this posed no problem: her only condition was that she be allowed to use her own backing singers, headed by Madeleine Bell. Interestingly, she opened with Dorothy Squires' (then) opener, "I Only Want To Laugh"—she too was in the audience, and led the standing ovation—and closed with Dalida's arrangement of "La Bamba". In between, the hilights of the evening were "My Colouring Book", a new Italian song called "Give Me Time", Burt Bacharach's "The Look Of Love", and of course "You Don't Have To Say You Love Me". The showstoppers on most nights were Charles Aznavour's "Yesterday When I Was Young" (which she would record in 1972), Luigi Tenco's "Senza parole" (which she sadly never recorded) and Jacques Brel's signature tune, "Ne me quitte pas", which she partly sang in flawless French, sending shivers down the spine. "The song is about fear and rejection," she told *Woman* magazine a few years later, "It's that first day at school feeling. Don't go away and leave me, Mama. It's the kind of feeling that can stay with you through life and become obsessive." As had happened at Beal Street East, it was standing room only every evening.

The Talk of the Town audiences may have loved Dusty's sweeping, highly emotive Continental ballads, but sometimes there was no pleasing some fans who, having been fed a giddy diet of Motown, were not quite ready for such overt sophistication. Even the ones who had rushed out in droves to buy "You Don't Have To Say You Love Me" and "Goin' Back" appeared to give a thumbs-down to Pietro Melfa's otherwise excellent "Give Me Time", when this was released as a single to coincide with Dusty's London triumph. Neither did DJs on both sides of the Atlantic help by persistently playing the B-side, "The Look Of Love", as a result of which the record stalled at Number 24 in the British charts, and at 22 in America. And yet, later on when her career was floundering, she confessed to disliking this type of venue, particularly in America, telling Jean Rook, "I hate the grey world of night clubs, stuffed with people eating and drinking—who hadn't come to see Dusty Springfield, but who'd just wondered, 'Say, Myron, who's on in the Blue Room tonight?"

By early June, Dusty was back in the studio filming her second television series, to be broadcast in the autum. The format was the same as before: six 30-minute shows produced by Stanley Dorman, with the emphasis this time placed on the sort of material she had performed in cabaret. Interspersed with the odd rowdy Motown classics and Italian standards were Hollywood show tunes: "My Foolish Heart", "Pick Yourself Up", "Let's Get Away From It All", "Do-Re-Mi", "If My Friends Could See Me Now", and Judy Garland's "By Myself". And if she had suffered one braggard across the waves—Buddy Rich—she now encountered another on home ground when "Velvet Fog" crooner Mel Torme guested, insisting on singing three songs instead of the customary one. Tom Jones, Engelbert Humperdinck and José Feliciano, on the other hand, she loved working with, though her favourite guest this time around was Scott Walker, who sang Jacques Brel's "Mathilde".

The television shows in the can, Dusty and Norma Tanega flew to Australia where she played a three-weeks season at Chequers, the 550-seat venue in Sidney whose owners were renowned for getting exactly who they wanted on account of the astronomical fees they offered—in Dusty's case, £5,000 a week. Australian Equity rules dictated that she would have to use in-house musicians, but when she arrived there was no bass player, so she paid The Echoes' Douggie Reece to fly out and join her. She was also assigned a personal hairdresser, celebrity stylist John Adams, who had little difficulty persuading her to ditch her wigs, on account of the heat, and let him work his magic on her locks. Rosemary Clooney was in town, and so enamoured of Adams' talent that she told friends she was thinking of inviting him to America to work exclusively for her. Dusty got there first. On her last night at Chequers, she handed Adams an envelope containing a first-class air ticket to London and promised to help him set up a salon there. Clooney meanwhile threatened to tear her hair out by the roots. Soon afterwards, Adams moved to Carnaby Street.

From Sydney, Dusty flew to New York to promote her latest American single, "What's It Gonna Be?". Then it was off to Bermuda for a series of cabaret engagements. By now, she was introducing "tribute medleys" into her shows: some evenings she would sing a fifteen-minute Aretha Franklin or Dionne Warwick selection, or if the evening called for a mellow, more relaxed setting she would pay homage to the *chanson*, or Peggy Lee— Dusty's readings of Charles Trenet's "I Wish You Love" and Peggy's "Mr Wonderful" were nothing short of amazing. She also introduced a comedy sketch which was high-camp at its most profound: wearing a wig of ringlets, a short polka-dot dress and pumps, she would be joined on stage by four mincing sailors while mimicking Shirley Temple—singing "Animal Crackers In My Soup" and "The Good Ship Lollipop" is a high-pitched voice in front of a screen where the real child star was performing these with the sound dubbed.

Dusty was in Bermuda when she learned that the new single had only just made the Top 40. It mattered little to her that there had been standing room only at her shows. She, who loved meeting people, would spend hours in her dressing room with adoring fans after a show—then go home and sink into the blackest depression, fretting over record sales. To her way of thinking she had suffered a flop on the eve of Philips releasing her third studio album, and she now was convinced now that this would bomb because the jazz-show tunes-soul-chanson material did not befit the "pop art" cover. This depicted her in monochrome, wearing a picture hat and mini skirt, standing knock-kneed and with an orange psychedelic bubble coming out of her mouth—asking by way of the album's title, *"Where Am I Going?"* "My last single was a dud," she told journalists, "And when the critics see this cover they'll think I'm taking the piss." It *was* a silly cover, albeit in keeping with the Flower Power times, but her request to have it changed was denied. Effectively, she was worrying over nothing. At the time of its release the album may have sold less copies than its predecessors, but contents wise it was better than all of them.

Where Am I Going? opens with Cissy Houston's "Bring Him Back", part-penned by Mort Shuman, who besides being responsible for some of Elvis Presley's biggest hits shared adaptation honours with Rod McKuen while introducing the works of Jacques Brel to the English speaking world—McKuen's adaptation of "Ne me quitte pas", with which Dusty is almost unrivalled save of course by Brel himself, is also here. "Don't Let Me Lose This Dream" and "I Can't Wait to See My Baby's Face" were Dusty's tribute to Aretha Franklin, though whereas Franklin tends to squawk them, Dusty at least makes a concerted effort to sing them properly. Next there are Evie Sands' "Take Me For A

Little While", Betty Everett's "Chained To A Memory", and Bobby Hebb's "Sunny" which Dusty had performed at Basin Street East. Upon hearing that Dionne Warwick had complained about her purloining her songs, Dusty "nicked" another— Bacharach and David's "They Long To Be Close To You", long before The Carpenters made it their own. After Chip Taylor's "Welcome Home" (not to be confused with the later Peters & Lee song of the same name) we have Alan Jay Lerner's "Come Back To Me", the pastiche which Yves Montand sings to Barbra Streisand in *On A Clear Day You Can See Forever*. "Broken Blossoms" is a traditional anti-war song rearranged by her brother Tom. And finally there is the title-track, which Dorothy Fields and Cy Coleman had written for Juliet Prowse to sing in *Sweet Charity*. Like "My Way", this is a "trooper" anthem associated with someone much older than twenty-eight: the lonely woman, alone on the shelf, her own worst enemy because she has screwed up every relationship so far and now finds herself atoning for her folly because, "No matter where I go, I meet myself there." All in all, a pretty eclectic collection.

For Dusty, 1968 proved a year of ups and downs, triumphs, cancellations, tantrums and mixed fortunes. Much of it was spent zipping back and forth across the Atlantic fulfilling cabaret engagements with her always seeming to be in the wrong place at the wrong time where invaluable promotions were concerned. She should have performed Bacharach and David's "The Look Of Love" at that year's Academy Awards—the song, which she sang over the soundtrack of the spook Bond film, *Casino Royale*, had been nominated for an Oscar, but at the last minute she backed out, declaring that she was far too busy to take up a whole evening singing just one song. A few years later she duetted on it with Mireille Mathieu, Dusty singing in English, Mireille in French. In Amsterdam, on 6 March, she ran foul of the promoters of the prestigious *Grand Gala du Disque* by acting the prima donna and making extraneous demands. Firstly she complained about the lack of rehearsal facilities. Next she demanded that more attention be afforded her than fellow contributor Vikki

Carr, declaring that Carr had spent less time in the charts than she had, therefore she was of less importance. Her outburst, peppered with expletives, was caught on camera and she was given her marching orders. Dusty unfairly blamed the whole fiasco on Vic Billings for booking her at the event in the first place, and came close to firing him.

More fireworks were anticipated later in the month when Dusty appeared on *Sunday Night At The London Palladium*— Buddy Rich was on the bill. The drummer sent a message to her dressing room saying that he wanted to bury the hatchet. Dusty's response was so did she—in the top of his head! Their respective managers thankfully kept them apart. Rich was even pencilled in as a guest for her third television series, until the producer realised that this might not be such a good idea. Entitled *It Must Be Dusty*, this one was aired on ATV and was a distinct comedown from its predecessors—badly produced and staged, and with too much emphasis on the black music as opposed to the more sophisticated material with which she had been wowing cabaret audiences. Also, Dusty had no say in the guest list—these were mostly B-listers, the exceptions being Scott Walker, Georgie Fame, and Julie Felix. A big scoop was wildman Jimi Hendrix, who against everyone's expectations and belief duetted with her on "Mockingbird", at one point plucking the guitar with his teeth. This performance aside, the critics were mostly disapproving, and as had happened with the Amsterdam fiasco, Vic Billings found himself taking the rap. This time Dusty did fire him—though so far as the press were told, the parting of the ways was amicable. Billings retaliated by serving her with a writ for £30,000 in estimated future commission earnings, but the matter was settled out of court when Dusty paid him £20,000. One of Billings' final jobs had been securing her £10,000 for her most unusual engagement so far—plugging Mother's Pride bread! In the 30-seconds commercial a tomboyish, wigless Dusty is seen pushing her cart along a narrow provincial street, singing "I'm a happy knocker-upper" while delivering loaves on the end of poles to the customer's bedroom windows!

In the June, Dusty released her sixteenth single, Clive Westlake's sublime "I Close My Eyes And Count To Ten", almost a *chanson* in that it was three melodies rolled into one, and one which Vic Billings had earmarked for Kiki Dee. After her recent small crop of failures she expected this one to bomb too, but it proved a deserved hit and a showpiece for future live appearances, reaching Number 5 in the charts. Its success coincided with Dusty signing a US contract with Atlantic Records, the idea being that she would record equally in Britain and America, with each company releasing the other's records. Intially, she was assigned to three albums. In the September, as part of the Atlantic deal—accompanied by hairdresser John Adams—Dusty flew to Memphis to work on her first album. Her self-esteem was at an all-time low, convinced as she was that her career was spinning out of control and veering towards disaster. It was time, she said, to sink or swim, to search for hew horizons. "I was seduced by the Great American Dream," she later told columnist Jean Rook, "I thought it would rekindle the challenge I'd lost here, and initially it did—until I got mixed up with their great record company conglomerates. You begin to feel like a tax write-off to the accountants you never even see—and in the awful sort of greed that settled in in the Seventies." Her fragile psyche cannot have been helped when she saw the American Studios, a cluster of delapidated buildings next to the Hertz Village black ghetto. The place had not seen a lick of paint in years, and was plagued with rats. But, she was told, if the place had been good enough for Aretha Franklin, who was she to argue?

Dusty had performed pure, unadulterated soul before, but she had never recorded an entire album of the genre. And who better to produce than the legendary Jerry Wexler? Atlantic Studios had been founded in 1947 by Herb Abramson and Ahmet Ertegun. During the next decade there big stars had been The Drifters. Wexler (1917-2008), accredited with coining the phrase rhythm and blues, had produced some of the best in the business, including Ray Charles and Bob Dylan. Dusty, he declared, belonged in the "blue-eyed soul" category currently occupied by

Sonny and Cher. He brought in ace engineer Tom Dowd, and assembled a fine group of musicians: The Memphis Cats comprised pianist Bobby Woods, guitarist Reggie Young, and bassist Tommy Cogbill—previously they had backed Elvis Presley and Wilson Pickett. Dusty initially disapproved of Cogbill, for no other reason than she had wanted John Paul Jones, who had accompanied her at the Talk of the Town. Jones, who could play just about every musical instrument known to man, was currently indisposed, having recently formed Led Zeppelin. It was Dusty who personally met with the Atlantic executives to plead with them, to make up with "foisting" Cogbill onto her, to at least offer the band a cotnract. They did, to the tune of $200,000, then a record signing for a new outfit.

As had happened when The Springfields had recorded in America, Dusty was given no say in her choice of material. Earlier in the year, at his Long Island home, Wexler had presented her with eighty songs and, not surprisingly for a perfectionist who prided herself in her eclectic repertoire, she had dismissed every single one. "Although she was ravishingly gorgeous, her doubts and insecurities had amounted to neurosis," Wexler recalled, well aware that any neurosis had been inflicted by himself by trying to force her to do something against his will. What he did not also add was how rudely he behaved towards her, of how this had led to innumerable in-studio rows which had culminated with her flinging a glass ashtray at him. Now, those same eighty songs were whittled down to twenty, and still she was dissatisfied. Neither did Wexler and his mouthy team help by persistently singing the praises of their golden girl, Aretha Franklin, leaving Dusty plagued with doubts that she would never be fit to follow in her footsteps—quite the opposite, for she ran rings around the over-loud, screeching American singer. "Why are you bothering to record me when you can't stop talking about *her*?" she complained at the time. Feeling intimidated, she supervised the orchestrations and the backing from The Sweet Temptations (one of these was Cissy Houston, the mother of Whitney), but refused to sing a note until Wexler had found her a studio away from "Arethaland"—resulting in the album's title, *Dusty In Memphis* becoming something of a misnomer. "All hell ensued," Wexler recalled, "The psychic struggle between Dusty and me was Machiavellian."

Some years later, Dusty defended herself against this at times obnoxious man. "What he didn't realise was how intimidated I was," she told BBC Radio One's *The Atlantic Story*, "If there's one thing that intimidates good singing, it's fear—allowing the natural critic within me to criticize a note *before* it even left my throat, which destroys the flow of anything!" And yet, though she had few good things to say about him over the coming months, it was Wexler who baptised her "The Great White Lady". "Dusty had the stigmata of perfectablity," Wexler recalled of the New York sessions in the BBC documentary, *Definitely Dusty*, "When she [finally] did perform she was afraid to let it go because her standards were so high, and it might not come out exactly right."

With Wexler still at the helm, but with a minimum of personnel, the recording of the album was transferred to a studio in New York. Because she had so had it drilled into her that she would never be in the same league as Aretha Franklin, Dusty went through a brief period hating the sound of her own voice—asking Wexler for so much track while laying down her vocals that, absolutely deafened by what came through the headphones, she had been *unable* to hear herself. She also caused the producer grief by insisting upon working in the early hours of the morning, at a time he felt he should have been at home in bed.

Whilst she was recording in America, Philips released her fourth studio album for them, *Dusty...Definitely*, co-produced by herself with Johnny Franz. Very much in the vein of *Where Am I Going?*, this had the novelty of being promoted as having a "black" side—the upbeat, Motown-style material—and a "white" side representing her cabaret work. Atlantic did not consider this sufficiently commercial for the kind of artiste they represented—truthfully, Wexler was against Philips' policy of allowing her to choose her own songs—therefore they renaged on their deal to release it Stateside. Dusty ranted and raved. What did *they* know about talent? Very little, it would appear, if they were foolish enough to reject this one, an excellent album, classy, way ahead of its time. It may have only reached Number 30 in the UK charts, but sales have more that made up for this since. Like the great song stylists she revered—Peggy Lee, Tony Bennett, Nat King Cole—not getting into the charts did not necessarily mean that their albums did not outsell the ones which did, in the long run.

Dusty...Definitely opens with The Temptations' "Ain't No Sun Since You've Been Gone", which she follows with Erma (sister of Aretha) Franklin's "Take Another Little Piece Of My Heart"—also covered by Janice Joplin. Bacharach and David's "Another Night" is next, a hit for Timi Yuro, whose "Hurt" Dusty had also considered recording. Also a hit for Elvis Presley, this would have suited her perfectly. Next up is Jerry Butler's "Mr Dream Merchant", and Diana Ross's "I Can't Give Back The Love I Feel For You". Closing Side One is Teddy Van's "Love Power". Side Two opens with Bacharach and David's "This Girl's In Love With You", a big hit for German chanteuse Hildegard Knef, though it was Herb Alpert who eventually took the male version to the top of the American charts. Knef had also had a hit with "No Sad Songs For Me", a phrase which Dusty incorporates into Dorothy Squires' "I Only Want To Laugh, an optimistic piece which runs nicely and succinctly into her definitive interpretation of Charles Aznavour's "Qui", adapted into English as "Who Will Take My Place?"—his "Yesterday When I Was Young" and "La bohéme" were already in her cabaret repertoire. Then comes her moving tribute to Peggy Lee with a stunning rendition of Randy Newman's torchy ballad, "I Think It's Gonna Rain Today". Peggy had just announced that she would be including this on her forthcoming album, *A Natural Woman*, which in itself caused a bust-up between Dusty and Jerry Wexler, who had co-written the title-track with Gerry Goffin and Carole King for Aretha Franklin to record the previous year. Dusty managed to get hold of a copy of the master tape, and told Wexler that, in her opinion, Peggy Lee could *snore* better than

Franklin would ever be able to sing! After Gilberto Gil's so-so "Morning", Dusty rounds off the proceedings with Sammy Cahn and Jimmy Van Heusen's "Second Time Around", which Frank Sinatra confessed had made him weep. All of her moods are represented on this album, yet just as we are regaining our breath after this last item, Dusty surprises us. The engineer had left the tape running when someone had wheeled the refreshments trolley into the studio, and Dusty was still seething from the latest blue with Wexler—and now we hear an almighty crash as she smashes its contents to smithereens against the wall!

This "dodgy" year ended on a positive note when Philips released John Hurley and Ronnie Wilkins' sensual, slightly risqué "Son-Of-A-Preacher-Man", taken from the forthcoming *Dusty In Memphis* album. Inasmuch as she had triumphed with the songs she had purloined from Dionne Warwick, so Dusty "got one over" on Aretha Franklin by getting a song she had rejected into the Top Ten on both sides of the Atlantic—delighted that Jerry Wexler's persistent boasting about his star protegee had backfired on him. Somehow, the tale of the eponymous Billy-Ray who falls for the girl who finds it hard to be good should have been more suited to Baptist minister's daughter Franklin, who did eventually record it. Dusty, the otherwise shy Catholic girl, gives a better delivery because she does so tongue-in-cheek, and with more restraint.

Dusty In Memphis was released with a fanfare of publicity in April 1969, with fans and critics alike hailing it one of her best. *Rolling Stone* could not praise it enough: "Most white female singers in today's music are still searching for music they can call their own. Dusty is not searching—she just shows up and she, and we, are better for it." Four decades later the magazine would still be applauding her "blazing soul and sexual honesty that transcended both race and geography", voting it Number 89 in their *500 Greatest Albums Of All Time* poll. Yet at the time it amounted to little more than a Pyrrhic victory for Dusty, selling considerably less copies than her previous albums—100,000 in America before being deleted—and failing to chart on both sides of the Atlantic. Rather than lift Dusty's spirits, it left her feeling more despondent than ever. The reason for its comparative failure had less to do with the album's content—her choice of material was first-class, as were the performances and arrangements—than Dusty's own reluctance to adequately promote it. Also, like many middle-of-the-road artistes who had risen to prominence in the early Sixties, a shift in musical trends had forced her career into an undeserved hiatus.

The album starts off with Cynthia Weill and Barry Mann's "Just A Little Lovin'", an optimistic, feelgood piece later covered by the songwriting duo's greatest champion, Barbra Streisand. Making love first thing in the morning, Dusty coquetishly proclaims, gives her a bigger buzz than coffee, and sets her in good stead for the rest of the day. If only everyone adopted the practice, she concludes, what a better world this would be! A nice thought, of course! Next comes the first of four Goffin-King songs, "So Much Love", which they had written for Ben E King. After "Son-Of-A-Preacher-Man" there is Randy Newman's "I Don't Want To Hear It Any More", the tale of the girl from the poor neighbourhood where everyone knows everyone's business, where gossip ruins clandestine love affairs. In Goffin and King's "Don't Forget About Me", Dusty sets her lover free in the hope that she will be fondly remembered, should their paths cross again. Eddie Hinton's "Breakfast In Bed" sees Dusty at her most sensual, and executes a neat spin on her biggest hit as she champions straightforward sex without its amorous complications: "Breakfast in bed and a kiss or three....you don't have to say you love me!" In gay clubs, this one would be much favoured by her sapphic sisters, and later the song would be less endearingly reprised by UB40 featuring Pretenders' singer Chrissie Hynde. "Just One Smile" returns Dusty to the pen of Randy Newman, and the number she shared with Gene Pitney. Nobody cares if she cries, so she will pretend that her lover is still here, though in the end she throws in the towel and concludes, "It's so hard to forget when your whole world you know is dying!"

Dusty had sung Brel, Aznavour, Charles Trenet (I Wish You Love), and Piaf just the once—"When The World Was Young". Now hes turned to Michel Legrand's "Les moulins de mon coeur", adapted into English by two more Streisand stalwarts, Alan and Marilyn Bergman. Noel Harrison had introduced the song over the soundtrack of *The Thomas Crown Affair*, but not nearly so well as this. Dusty's reading strongly adheres to the version recorded by French chanteuse Frida Boccara: breathy, emotive, entirely convincing as she uses poetic, psychedelic imagery to describe her inner turmoil following the break-up of yet another relationship. Life does not get much brighter in Burt Bacharach's "In The Land Of Make Believe", the weakest song on the album which sees Dusty emulating Blossom Dearie and straining in an uncustomarily squeaky voice: the lover is far away, perhaps gone for good, but she can still pretend that he/she is still here and that they are kissing in their long-dead paradise— for as long as she keeps up the pretence, they will always be together. And as with *Where Am I Going?*, *Dusty In Memphis* closes on an even more pessimistic note. With Goffin and King's "No Easy Way Down" she presents us with a "can't-do-right-for-doing-wrong" pastiche of self pity—the fact that one might *think* one has attained the giddy heights of love, in the real world there is no such thing as that crock of gold at the rainbow's end, just one more disappointment such as the one in "I Can't Make It Alone", Goffin and King's final contribution to the album. Here, Dusty begs the lover she hurt to forgive her and reach out to save her dying soul—for no other reason than she can no longer cope with the pain of loneliness.

For Dusty, things appeared to be going from bad to worse. 1969 was promised to be her busiest year ever—a supposedly non-stop round of tours and recording sessions. The comparative failure of *Dusty In Memphis* put paid to this. During the spring she toured North America and Canada, promoting "Windmills Of Your Mind". The single barely scraped into the *Billboard* Top 40, and though the first few dates sold out fairly quickly, attendances for the rest of the tour were poor—down to less than 50 per cent in some venues. A campus tour for the autumn was cancelled, also a cabaret season at New York's Americana Club. Dusty also lost her favourite backing singer. Madeleine Bell, a fine artiste in her own right, had joined up with singer-songwriter Roger Cook, Alan Parker and Herbie Flowers to form Blue Mink: starting with their racial harmony anthem, "Melting Pot", the group would enjoy seven UK Top 30 hits over the next four years. Disgruntled—there would be little contact between them from now on—Dusty returned to London where, pleased to be going back to the BBC, she taped her next eight-part television series, *Decidedly Dusty*, to begin broadcasting in the September.

This series was a distinct improvement on Dusty's last. Back to being allowed to choose her own guests, she plumped for Jimmy Ruffin and her favourite comedienne, Lamb Chop ventriloquist Shari Lewis. Her special guest in one show was Danny La Rue, who impersonated her singing "I Just Don't Know What To Do With Myself". For the final show, the producers had wanted Lulu, the joint winner (with France's Frida Boccara, the Netherlands' Lenny Kuhr, and Spain's Salomé) of that year's *Eurovision Song Contest*. Dusty requested Boccara (1940-96), a magnificent chanteuse who died tragically young, and who brought the house down with "Un jour, un enfant". A few years later, when preparing a television spectacular with Juliet Prowse and Burt Bacharach, Dusty would ask for Boccara but instead be given Mireille Mathieu. The trio would deliver an electrifying ten-minute tribute to The Beatles. To coincide with the series, Philips released "Am I The Same Girl?", which peaked at a disappointing Number 43 in the charts. Dusty blamed the record company for bringing it out at the wrong time, though there was hardly a right time—when she was busy filming television specials in Europe, she was zipping back and forth across the Atlantic to work on her next album.

In November 1969, Atlantic put out "A Brand New Me", taken from *From Dusty...With Love*, the last time her name would be used in an album title. Some years later, this would appear in the *Guardian*'s *1,000 Albums To Hear Before Yor Die* list. The single reached Number 25 in the US charts, prompting Atlantic to change the album's title to *A Brand New Me*. Dusty threw a fit and dropped the song from her repertoire. Next, in an expletives charged tirade, she turned on Jerry Wexler when he suggested another recording session in Memphis: she would not be working again here, or in New York, *or* with any of the musicians from the *Dusty In Memphis* sessions. She also flatly refused to have anything to do with pianist Bobby Woods, who she accused of homophobia. Some years later, speaking to biographer Lucy O'Brien, Woods confessed that he had had reservations about her "sexual reputation". "It was a kinda icky situation," he said, "I didn't want to get too close to it....In the country where I came from, if someone found out someone was homosexual you either got hung or run out of town." Eight years on, in Los Angeles and echoing similar comments made by Elizabeth Taylor, Dusty would tell a reporter from *Gay News,* "There's a very strong anti-gay feeling here, which is extraordinary in an industry which is 75 per cent gay. Because industry heads are very anti-gay it's very tough for most gay people and difficult to speak out....I respect gay people. That doesn't make me one, and that doesn't *not* make me one. But I have a gay following and I'm grateful for it." Little wonder then, when faced with such hypocrisy and prejudice, that Dusty sometimes had a short fuse.

The ten tracks were recorded at the Sigma Sound Studios, Philadelphia, at the end of 1969 and the album released in America in January 1970—in England, it retained its original title and came out in January. It was a concept album of sorts, the first Dusty had done where all the songs came from the same production team, headed by songwriter-producers Kenny Gamble and Leon Gamble, virtually unknown when they worked with her, though with her soul connections she had heard of them— they famously went on to work with The Three Degrees. Today, the album is regarded as a curiosity item with only hardcore fans knowing most of the songs, a shame because it is quite good. "Joe" is one of the nicest she performed at this time, as is "Let's Talk It Over" which has her backed with a gospel-style choir,

The Sweethearts of Sigma. She should have had a major hit on her hands, but as the decade drew to a close, she was faced with an inconsolable dilemma. Philips were reluctant to promote her US releases while she was working in America for Atlantic, and vice-versa. Though most of her shows were sell-outs whichever side of the Atlantic she happened to be on, it was this constantly being in the wrong place at the wrong time which helped bring down the curtain on Dusty Springfield's commercial career when she was just thirty years old, though as an artiste she would of course shine until the very end.

Chapter Five

Ne me quitte pas....

How can I be sure, in a world that's constantly changing?" Dusty asked, in September 1970. Written by Felix Cavaliere and Eddie Brigati, "How Can I Be Sure?" had been introduced by The Young Rascals. Dusty had never heard of them or their version: during a trip to Paris she has heard Nicoletta (Nicole Grisoni) singing the French version, "Je ne pense qu'a t'aimer, on the juke box. Born in 1944, Nicoletta had a similar voice to Dusty's—indeed, Ray Charles, who covered her "Il est mort le soleil", said, "There are only two women alive today with black voices—Nicoletta and Dusty Springfield." Someone called the chanteuse, and it was agreed that Dusty would be permitted to sing the same arrangement, complete with accordions. As such it is one of her finest interpretations. She promoted it on *The Morecambe & Wise Show*, and the record reached Number 35 in the charts and with more airplay almost certainly would have gone higher. Later there would be cover versions by David Cassidy and Gloria Estefan. The Nicoletta version, however, has sold the most copies.

Sadly, Dusty's world was already changing. In a musical environment where success was measured in revolutions per minute, her fabulous hit-parade run had more or less ended after less than a decade. Had she readily accepted this—as most of her middle-of-the-road contemporaries had been compelled to—she might have survived better over the next thirty years. Tom Jones, Peggy Lee, Frank Sinatra, Vikki Carr, Kathie Kirby, Engelbert Humperdinck, Sandie Shaw and dozens more rarely enjoyed chart success once the Seventies dawned, yet they were no less successful on the cabaret-theatre circuit. Most too became album stars, selling many more copies than the so-called megastars of today without even *getting* into the charts. Edith Piaf and Nana Mouskouri, who each had just one chart entry in Britain, have at the time of writing sold over 400 million albums between them. For Dusty, however, more popular than ever with audiences at this time, it was almost as if it had to be the charts or nothing at all.

Her third album for Atlantic, *Faithful*, was abandoned—the aborted material would be added to the 1999 reissue of *Dusty In Memphis*. The next one, *See All Her Faces*, was released in Britain only. Its successor, *Cameo*, was released in the US on the ABC Dunhill label in 1973 and depite above average material from the pens of Melissa Manchester, Barry Manilow, and Barry Mann and Cynthia Weill received virtually no airplay or mention in the music press. Dusty had hated making it. "They wanted me to record material *they* had selected, she told *Billboard* magazine, "I was terribly galled that they'd done some tracks without even asking me what key. I became terribly unco-operative and dug in my heels. I wanted out." Dorothy Squires, who she had met through their mutual friend Danny La Rue—the two even swapped dresses!—told me, "Most of the songs Dusty was forced to sing in those days were second rate. A singer has her own particular style which she likes to stick to. They wouldn't have got away with telling Bassey or myself what to sing. Dusty was too soft with them."

Critics could not help but observe that some of the songs had been given portentous titles: "Mixed Up Girl", "Let Me Down Easy", "Nothing Is Forever", "Girls It Ain't Easy", and her flawless reading of Aznavour's "Yesterday When I Was Young" which was given pride of place in her opening night at the Talk of The Town on 4 December. Dusty was suffering from the flu, and advised by her doctor to cancel. Manager Bernard Delfont would not hear of this: she struggled valiantly through an excellent 65-minute set, coughing and sipping water between songs, and even gave a couple of encores. The next morning, however, she received a call from Harold Fielding, the first of many managers during her "wilderness" years: the rest of the four-weeks season had been cancelled. Dusty subsequently sued Delfont for £10,000 in lost earnings, and won.

Things appeared to be looking up when Dusty recorded Glen Larson and Stu Philips' theme for two *Six-Million Dollar Man* television movies. Her voice was in tremendous form, and it was a pretty good tune—only the lyrics were naff. At around the same time she began work on her second ABC Dunhill album, but the sessions were inexplicably abandoned. Some of this material would be released on the 2001 compilation, *Beautiful Soul*.

Having ended her relationship with Norma Tanega, Dusty relocated to Los Angeles—she said to get away from the British tabloids, forever on the lookout for exclusives on her private life. Speaking to the Ray Connolly of London's *Evening Standard*, and in an act which was quite out of character for her, back in 1970 she had confessed to being promiscuous and the guilt this brought, adding, "I don't leap into bed with someone new every night, but I can be very unfaithful. It's fun while its happening, but not fun afterwards because I'm filled with self-recrimination." In 1973 she would go one step further, telling the *Los Angeles Free Press*, "I mean, people say that I'm gay, gay, gay, gay, gay, gay, gay, gay. I'm not anything. I basically want to be straight. I go from men to women and I don't give a shit. The catchphrase is: I can't love a man. Now, that's my hang-up. To love, to go to bed—fantastic. But to love a man is my prime ambition. They frighten me!" And that was that, making one wonder what all the "Is-she-isn't-she?" fuss had been about. Nothing had changed—she was still the same Dusty, after all!

The newspapers reported tales of drug abuse and alcohol dependency, hospitalisations due to self-harming incidents. Friends who stuck by her while she was alive have since her death recounted her drinking sprees, and "cutting" incidents which they believe to have been linked to the attention-seeking hand-burning of her childhood. They have also told of the suicide attempts—the slashed wrists, overdoses, and threats to fling herself off balconies. Some of these incidents happened, some were buffered up to appear more serious than they really were. Dusty certainly went through a very bad patch in 1983, becoming a victim of domestic violence which resulted in doctors temporarily certifying her a manic depressive. In April of this year, at an Alcoholics Anonymous meeting in Los Angeles, she fell in with an unsavoury crowd and struck up a friendship with Teda Bracci, an unstable bit-part actress who had recently played a mental patient in the film, *Frances*, a depressing saga if ever there was one telling the story of lobotomised movie star Frances Farmer. The relationship developed, and seven months later the couple "married" at the San Fernando ranch of Helene Sellery, another AA member—the party guests were all from an infamous local rehab centre. Dusty, the bride, in a rare moment of lapsed fashion sense wore a floor-length "chez Oxfam" white meringue gown and white silk stetson, while the "groom" wore black. Their first row occurred during the journey home, when the now-teetotal Dusty learned that Bracci had sneaked a bottle of champagne into the reception. Their last was not long afterwards when, apparently after several nasty attacks by her partner, she was hospitalised after Bracci hit her in the face with a saucepan, smashing her cheek and knocking out several teeth. Not to be outdone, Dusty hit her over the the head with a skillet—exit Teda Bracci. She told Kris Kirk,

> I was beaten up more than once by the same
> person, and the second time I experienced what
> battered wives often come up against, where
> they're not only afraid to talk because they'll get
> beaten up again. But the relation ship was so
> disapproved of anyway that people turned round
> and said, 'We told you so, you should never have
> married her in the first place.' I've been through it
> and if I can do anything to help there, I will.

Plastic surgery performed at the Cedars Sinai Hospital gave
Dusty a new look: her face emerged thinner, almost emaciated at
first, her cheekbones, chin and nose more pronounced. She had
also ditched most of her wigs, and cut down on the mascara—the
black stuff which she once said she hardly ever washed off had
been eschewed for a more subtle deep purple and magenta. In
America, she became involved with several refuges for battered
women, performing in charity concerts to rais funds—this was
when she was not raising money for her animal charities,
including one which rescue kodiak bears. At this trying time she
also provided backing vocals for "Snowbird" songstress Anne
Murray's album, *Together*, and Elton John's *Caribou*.

In 1978, Dusty recorded *It Begins Again* for Atlantic.
Completed at the Cherokee Studios in West Hollywood, the
album was produced by Roy Thomas Baker, though for Dusty
things would not be beginning again for a while. Her 1979 UK
album, *Living Without Your Love*, fared slightly better but still
did not chart. Philips promoted it as her comeback release,
though she was quick to remind journalists that she had not really
been anywhere. Neither, she said, was doing it for the money. "If
I had to do it for that alone, I'd breed cats," she snapped at one
journalist. Again, some of the songs were portentous and most
especially appreciated by her legion of gay fans: "Be Somebody",
"Closet Man", "Save Me, Save Me"—and "I'm Coming Home
Again".

This was another year of mixed fortunes. Sell-out concerts at London's Drury Lane Theatre were followed by provincial cancellations owing to poor advertising and therefore poor ticket sales. Though distressed about this, Dusty made light of the situation—appearing on the BBC's *Pebble Mill At One* wearing her "funeral" attire of Portuguese *fadista*'s black veil. At the end of the year, however, she gave a spectacular concert at London's Royal Albert Hall—one of her finest later recitals, if not the finest of her career. Piaf had done *Olympia 60,* Judy Garland *Carnegie Hall 61*, Dorothy Squires *Palladium 70*. All had been recorded for posterity, and sold millions of copies worldwide. All three performances had taken place in the face or wake of extreme adversity—Dusty's too, for it was the day before her father's funeral, and when she was still getting over losing her mother to lung cancer. OB had been found dead of a suspected heart-attack at his home.

The Royal Albert Hall concert constituted a charity performance, in front of a frosty and very rude Princess Margaret, on behalf of the Invalid Children's Aid Society. Introduced by a sneering, condescending Russell Harty, Dusty bounced on to the stage wearing a sparkling white top and trousers, and opened with "I Close My Eyes And Count To Ten". Next up was "We Are Family", within which she emphasised the line, "All my sisters and me!" Around 90 per cent of the capacity crowd were sapphic or gay and Dusty played to these, as did the camera, completely ignoring the royal patron. All the big hits were there, each greeted with a bigger storm of applause than the last, and insasmuch as the fans were not interested in Princess Margaret, neither was Dusty. The crunch came after "All I See Is You" when Dusty quite inoccuously pronounced, "It's nice to see that all the royalty is not confined to the royal box!" The Princess was clearly not amused and walked out—returning after what one member of the theatre's staff described as "a fag and gin break" to catch the last two songs. Here, Dusty had her revenge when she glanced up and saw the Princess chatting to her lady-in-waiting. Disappearing into the wings for a lightning change into a beautiful tailed lilac trouser-suit, she walked back on and, stepping over a carpet of multicoloured carnations, began her penultimate song, "Quiet please—there's a lady on the stage!" This was not just her tribute to all the great tragic female singers of the past, but Dusty's inadvertent way of telling this other lady to shut up and not be so rude—that the lady standing in the spotlight might be past her best, but that she was still entitled to a little respect. This show of bad manners continued after the show, when Princess Margaret congratulated everyone who had been involved with the production—and arrogantly strode straight past Dusty, whose manager had just handed her a cheque for £8,000 which Dusty had raised!

There was more. The next day, Dusty received a letter from St James' Palace—a pre-typed apology for the "insults" she had levelled at the Queen, with a space for her signature! Such was her naivety that she signed the paper and returned it. The show had been taped for broadcast over the Christmas period, but now the BBC dropped it from their schedule. The hilarious end to this upsetting episode was recalled by Dusty's biographer, Sharon Davis, in 2008: "Known by the nickname Yvonne in the gay fraternity, a news item in the *Daily Mail* in 2007 suggested that Princess Margaret 'was rumoured to have had affairs with lovers including Peter Sellers and, more improbably, Dusty Springfield.'" Neither was it the first time that Dusty had "offended" royalty: the previous year she had half-jokingly told *Gay News*, "I'm having a three-way with Princess Anne and one of her horses."

Had Dusty taken a leaf out of the Piaf-Judy-Squires book and concentrated on giving tremendous performances instead of worrying about record sales, her career might have gone on to reach unprecedented heights. In 1981 she signed a contract in the US with 20th Century Records, and the following year released an album, *White Heat*. Most fans were more interested in the sleeve than the content: the reverse depicted her wearing a motorcycle helmet, it was alleged at the time to conceal the bruises inflicted by Teda Bracci. Arguably the worst album she ever made was the record company's attempts to use Dusty to cash in on the current Hi Energy gay disco craze which even the sultry Eartha Kitt had conquered. For Dusty, it was just another flop.

In 1985, Dusty returned to the UK, where she gave the previously mentioned interview for the *Daily Express*'s acid-tongued columnist Jean Rook, who observed with her usual lack of tact, "At first startling glance, she looks like a terrorist with a built-in hood. Or an ancient Greek death mask. Her mouth is a blood red gash. Her make-up looks bullet-proof." And top of Rook's agenda—Dusty's sexuality. To say that the interview was an ordeal may be an understatement, though there would be more to come by the end of this particular visit to her homeland. Hippodrome owner Peter Stringfellow had assigned her to a £100,000 one-album-three-singles deal with his Hippodrome Records label, along with engagements at his clubs up and down the country—concluding with a season at the Hippodrome itself, a mecca for for the gay community. The most he got in the end was a one-off television appearance on the BBC's *Wogan*, promoting her new single, "Sometimes Like Butterflies". This had originally featured on the flipside of Donna Summer's "Finger On The Trigger", and for a woman whose fanbase was so predominantly gay, the last thing Dusty wanted was to be associated with a woman who had publicly declared that AIDS was God's punishment on gay men, a statement which almost irreparably damaged Summer's career. "I think Peter and I make an explosive combination," Dusty said at the time, though when the record flopped and she returned to America with her tail tucked firmly between her legs, she was singing a different tune. "Peter knew fuck all about the record industry," she told a waiting press conference, "My relationship with him was one of the incidents that made me so fed up with the business, I nearly gave it up for good." Stringfellow defended himself by saying that this was indeed true, that he knew very little about the record indistry—but enough to know that it was impossible for any artiste to have a hit with a record they refused to promote, as

Dusty had done. And the problem had of course arisen over the *choice* of record, which had been Dusty's decision alone.

The tabloids, and even Dusty herself at times, were suggesting that maybe she was all washed up. Then, in 1987, when Vicki Wickham took over as her manager, came an offer to work with The Pet Shop Boys—an idea originally suggested by Peter Stringfellow, and impolitely dismissed. This time the opportunity came by way of Neil Tennant, a fervent Dusty fan, who asked her to duet with them on their new single, "What Have I Done To Deserve This?", and also appear in the promotional video. The record reached Number 2 in the British and US charts, though whether by way of merit or on account of its curiosity value may be a matter for conjecture. With the flat, tuneless voices of Tennant and Chris Lowe, and with Dusty only slightly improving matters with her "Since you went away" segments, it was vastly inferior to her recent singles which had flopped—though her subsequent work with The Pet Shop Boys would show a marked improvement when their voices were kept out of the proceedings. "I'm really grateful to The Pet Shop Boys", she said in a BBC Radio One interview, "And I feel embarrassed to say that. It sticks in my craw to be grateful, but I am because they had the faith in me that I didn't have."

Much, much better was Dusty's duet, "Something In Your Eyes", with an almost inaudible Richard Carpenter for his *Time* album, Carpenter's first solo outing since the death of his sister Karen. The single reached Number 12 in the US Adult Contemporary Chart. The promotional video was also interesting: Dusty lip-synchs the song while leaning, Judy-style, against the upright piano. She also recorded a duet with B J Thomas: "As Long As We Got Each Other" was the theme from the American sitcom, *Growing Pains*. Then, in January 1988 she hit the jackpot when Philips put out *The Silver Collection*, a for once well-publicised retrospective of her halycon days. Within a month of its release, the 22-track album achieved gold status, bringing the comment from *Melody Maker*, "If Dusty Springfield didn't exist, it would naturally be necessary to invent her."

The album's success prompted Dusty to leave America for good. Unable to bring her beloved cats to Britain on account of the strict quarantine laws, she relocated to Holland where this was possible, renting a cramped flat in Amsterdam. Zipping back and forth to London she appeared on numerous chat shows, setting a precedent by always having a friend close at hand. Toying nervously with her fingers, she would persistently glance to the wings—which she admitted she could not see on account of her acute myopia—as if in search of approval that the interview was going well. One with Clive Anderson went badly. Anderson seemed interested only in drawing attention to his non-funny jokes, while the (unseen) props man instructed the audience when to laugh and Dusty refused to sing. "Never again," she said afterwards. Michael Aspel, on the other hand, coaxed out of her a rip-roaring "I Only Want To Be With You", treated her (as indeed he treated all his guests) kindly and with respect, and she reciprocated with unusual candour when asked about her recent addictions:

> There's nothing funny about a drunken woman, and nothing funnyabout a very stoned woman....I wouldn't recommend joining that particular club. [Stopping] is not a matter of willpower, it's just a matter of finding that you dislike yourself so much and you're behaving like a complete creep. Some people never realise that about themselves....It's very easyto stop drinking and doing drugs. It's not easy to stay stopped.

In February 1989, Dusty released her second, technically and vocally more satisfactory collaboration with The Pet Shop Boys—"Nothing Has Been Proved" was used on the soundtrack of the film, *Scandal,* which recounted the John Profumo-Christine Keeler-Mandy Rice Davies hoohah which in 1963, when Dusty was starting out as a solo artiste, had brought down the Macmillan government. The record, a lengthy one which saw

Dusty working with later Marianne Faithfull favourite Angelo Badalamenti, gave her all the vocals this time (The Pet Shop Boys intermittently pronounced the word "scandal") and reached Number 16 in the UK charts, her first big solo hit since 1968's "I Close My Eyes And Count To Ten". As had happened with her Shirley Temple sketch, the promotional video showed Dusty, gloved and clad in purple, sporting a new spiky hairstyle while performing in front of monochrome newsreel footage of the Profumo affair. The single also saw her making a welcome return to *Top Of The Pops*, and an allegedly not so welcome reunion with *Ready, Steady, Go!*'s Cathy McGowan, who asked her during a local television news report, "What does it feel like to be a superstar again?" As if she had ever been anything else!

"Nothing Has Been Proved" was one of the tracks on Dusty's new album, *Reputation*, released in June 1990—her first for Parlophone, the label responsible for Cilla Black's biggest hits. Part-produced by The Pet Shop Boys, it had been recorded over an 18-months period and peaked at Number 38 in the charts, selling 80,000 copies in its first month. The second single from the album, "In Private", reached Number 14. Dusty was back! She also returned to London, moving in with secretary Pat Rhodes and her husband until she could find a place of her own—for the next six months, her preoccupation would be in ensuring that she never missed a day visiting her cats in quarantine. Eventually, she moved into The Granary, part of the Frogmill Court complex at Hurley, in Berkshire.

Dusty hit the headlines in 1991 following a sketch in ITV's *The Bobby Davro Show* wherein the comic had parodied her, wearing high heels and a cheap wig, staggering across the stage, swigging from a bottle while slurring the words to "What Have I Done To Deserve This?" Dusty was upset, but may not have taken the matter further had it not been for a call from Dorothy Squires, who over the years had had more than her share of similar attacks. Dorothy told me, "I told her, 'Sue the hell out of them, Dusty. Once you let these bastards get away with robbing you of your dignity, they just keep on doing it.'" Oddly, it was not Davro she sued but the television company. She had *had* a drink problem, she confessed, but for eight years now not one drop of alcohol had passed her lips. The court awarded her £75,000 in damages, and ordered ITV to make a public apology.

In October 1993, Dusty repaired her "rift" with Cilla Black— if indeed there had ever been one—when Cilla was putting together an album feting her thirty years in show business. *Through The Years* was a collection of duets with friends and colleagues, and Dusty's contribution was *Heart & Soul*, which was also released as a single. The following year, Columbia this time put out what would be her final album, *A Very Fine Love*, produced by Tom Shapiro. Recorded in Nashville, where The Springfields had made their first American album, she had wanted to call it *Dusty In Nashville*, but the record company talked her out of it, claiming that fans and the media would be expecting a country album. Released in the UK in June 1995, it barely squeezed into the Top 40.

Dusty had been feeling run down for a while, and when she returned home from America she consulted her doctor, who discovered an abnormality in her breast. She was immediately sent to see a specialist at the Royal Marsden Hospital, who discovered cancer—fairly advanced, though not too advanced to effect a cure. She was immediately put on a course of chemotherapy, and the fact that this did not make her lose her hair or too much weight enabled her to keep her illness a secret from all but her closest friends. The news finally hit the press in November 1994, why which time doctors at the Royal Marsden had given her an "above average" chance of survival. She carried on working as usual, promoting the new album. There were appearances on *The Edna Everage Show*, and on BBC2's *Later With Jools Holland*, where she plugged a new single, "Where Is A Woman To Go?"—her "backing singers" were fellow guests Sinead O'Connor and Alison Moyet. She made a fleeting appearance on ITV's breakfast programme, where she spoke candidly about her cancer diagnosis to Lorrain Kelly and publicly thanked the Royal Marsden for looking after her. Not long afterwards, portentously performing George and Ira Gershwin's "Someone To Watch Over Me", she made a 60-seconds television commercial for life assurance. Her swansong was a taped a segment for *Des O'Connor Tonight*—some years earlier, they had clowned around while duetting on "Messing About On The River".

Early in 1996, Dusty's cancer returned with a vengeance—the disease had now spread to her bones. Over the next six months she underwent yet more chemotherapy, and surprisingly for one known to favour looking on the black side, fought valiantly from her corner. Her three closest friends—Pat Rhodes, Vicki Wickham and backing-singer Simon Bell—were asked to sign confidentiality agreements promising not to discuss her illness, or her private life after her death. Wickham would subsequently pen a kiss-and-tell, *Dancing With Demons*. Dusty began planning her funeral. A lapsed Cathlic, she wanted to atone by having a priest officiate at her service, after which she would be privately cremated—her ashes would be divided into two urns, one to be interred within the local churchyard so that fans could visit, the other to be scattered into the Atlantic from one of her favourite beauty spots, the Cliffs of Moher, in County Clare. Her possessions would be sold, and the proceeds donated to various friends and animal charities. In the meantime, to ensure that she would have the very best in medical care, she assigned her future royalties to the Prudential Insurance Company for £1.25 million—effectively a loan which in time would be paid back.

Dusty's friends fiercely protected her from the outside world, inasmuch as her fans only learned how ill she really in February 1998 was when she failed to turn up at the BRITs, where she was to have presented Icelandic singer Bjork with an award. Within hours, dozens of reporters were camped in the forecourt outside her Berkshire home, along with hundreds of anxious fans. This was almost a repeat of what had happened to Freddie Mercury, in 1991, when news had broken that he had been dying from AIDS. There was no question of Dusty staying here now, and shortly afterwards she moved into a large rented house set in extensive grounds at Harpsden Bottom, Henley-on-Thames. The property was enclosed by an electric fence, assuring her of complete privacy.

On 14 April, two days before her 59th birthday, she tuned in to the television news to learn that Dorothy Squires had died of lung cancer, aged eighty. The woman generally regarded—also by Dusty—as Britain's greatest ever female singer was buried in Streatham, London. Dusty, who still had one of Dorothy's dresses in her closet, sent flowers to the funeral. Three days later she received word that Paul McCartney's wife, Linda, had also succumbed to the disease.

In the May, doctors at the Royal Marsden gave Dusty just three months to live. Surrounded by friends and loved ones, she rallied a little and soldiered on for a good deal longer, so much so that fans switching on their radios in anticipation of hearing the worst came to the conclusion that, as before, she had been given the all clear. They realised this was not so when, on 30 December, her name was published in the New Year's Honours List. She, who had never held much faith with royalty since being snubbed by Princess Margaret, had been awarded the OBE. The grim news was that she might not live to personally collect the award from Buckingham Palace. Arrangements were therefore made for Vicki Wickham to collect it on her behalf and present it to her at the Royal Marsden.

A few days after receiving her OBE, Dusty returned to Henley. Refusing to sleep in her bedroom, between bouts of consciousness she held court in her beautifully furnished living room. It was here, at 10.43 pm on Tuesday 2 March—the very day she should have gone to Buckingham Palace, that she slipped away in her sleep.

*   *   *   *   *

Dusty's funeral, on Friday 12 March 1999, befitted the noble, beautiful person she had been—a day which, with her frequently warped sense of humour, would have amused her because it was

Red Nose Day. She had jokingly remarked how she had wanted to stop the traffic and bring Henley to a standstill, and this is exactly what happened. The town centre was cordoned off as hundreds of fans began arriving to pay their last respects. In the gentle drizzle, some fell to their knees behind the crash-barriers, to which had been attached tiny bunches of wild flowers. The celebrity mourners included Dusty's brother Tom, Lulu, The Pet Shop Boys, Elvis Costello, Madeleine Bell, Julie Felix and Kiki Dee. Floral tributes had been sent by Sandie Shaw, Cilla Black, Dionne Warwick, The Rolling Stones, and Burt Bacharach.

Years before, during a visit to Rome, a friend had showed Dusty some old footage of Mario Lanza's funeral, where the great tenor's casket had woven its way through the city's streets in a glass-sided antique carriage, drawn by liveried black horses. Anyone visiting Henley and not knowing what had happened might have been excused for thinking that the crowds were saying farewell to a royal personage, and in a way they were. Within the carriage, the name DUSTY was spelled out in pink and white flowers, and as the coffin was carried into the Parish Church of St Mary The Virgin, Dusty's recording of "You Don't Have To Say You Love Me" was relayed through loud speakers. During the service, Simon Bell, who had helped nurse her through her final illness, sang "The Wind Beneath My Wings". For many, however, the most heartbreaking moment was when Dusty's voice rang out again as the coffin left the church to a loud applause from the crowd.

"I think I'm going back......

Dusty Springfield

Solo Discography: 1960s Vinyl

1963
I Only Want To Be With You/ Once Upon A Time
Philips BF1292

1964
Stay Awhile/ Something Special
Philips BF1313

I Only Want To Be With You: I Only Want To Be With You; He's Got Something; Twenty-Four Hours From Tulsa; Every Day I Have To Cry
(EP) Philips BE12560

A Girl Called Dusty: Mama Said; You Don't Own Me; Do Re Mi; When The Lovelight Starts Shining Thru His Eyes; My Colouring Book; Mockingbird; Twenty-Four Hours From Tulsa; Nothing; Anyone Who Had A Heart; Will You Love Me Tomorrow; Wishin' & Hopin'; Baby Don't You Know
(LP) Philips BL7594

I Just Don't Know What To Do With Myself/ My Colouring
Book
Philips BF1348

Aud dich nur wart'ich immerzu/ Warten und hoffen
German release, no other details

Dusty: Can I Get A Witness; All Cried Out; Wishin' & Hopin'; I
Wish I'd Never Loved You
(EP) Philips BE12564

Tento so che poi mi passa/ Stupido, stupido
Italian release, no other details

Losing You/ Summer Is Over
Philips BF1369

Tu che ne sai/ Di fronte all'amore
Italian release, no other details

O Holy Child/ Jingle Bells (with The Springfields)
Philips BF1381

1965
Your Hurtin' Kinda Love/ Don't Say It Baby
Philips BF1396

Dusty In New York: Live It Up; I Want Your Love Tonight; I
Wanna Make You Happy; Now That You're My Baby
(EP) Philips 12572

In The Middle Of Nowhere/ Baby Don't You Know
Philips BF1418

Mademoiselle Dusty: Demain tu peux changer; L'été est fini; Je
ne peux pas t'en vouloir; Reste encore un instant

(EP) Philips BE12579

Some Of Your Loving/ I'll Love You For A While
Philips BF1430

Everything's Coming Up Dusty: Won't Be Long; Oh No! Not My Baby; Long After Midnight Is All Over; La Bamba; Who Can I Turn To; Doodlin'; If It Don't Work Out; That's How Heartaches Are Made; It Was Easier To Hurt Him; I've Been Wrong Before; I Can Hear You; I Had A Talk With My Man; Packin' Up
(LP) Philips RBL1002

1966
Little By Little/ If It Hadn't Been For You
Philips BF1466

You Don't Have To Say You Love Me/ Every Ounce Of Strength
Philips BF1482

Goin' Back/ I'm Gonna Leave You
Philips BF1502

All I See Is You/ Go Ahead On
Philips BF1510

Golden Hits: I Only Want To Be With You; I Just Don't Know What To Do With Myself; In The Middle Of Nowhere; Losin' You' All Cried Out; Some Of Your Lovin'; Wishin' & Hopin'; My Colouring Book; Little By Little; You Don't Have To Say You Love Me; Goin' Back; All I See Is You
(LP) Philips BL7737

1967
I'll Try Anything/ The Corrupt Ones
Philips BF1553

Give Me Time/ The Look Of Love
Philips BF1577

What's It Gonna Be/ Small Town Girl
Philips BF1608

Where Am I Going: Bring Him Back; Don't Let Me Lose This
Dream; I Can't Wait Until I See My Baby's Face; Take Me For
A Little While; Chained To A Memory; Sunny; They Long To
Be Close To You; Welcome Home; Come Back To Me; If You
Go Away; Broken Blossoms; Where Am I Going
(LP) Philips BL7820

1968
I Close My Eyes And Count To Ten/ No Stranger Am I
Philips BF1682

If You Go Away: If You Go Away; Magic Garden; Sunny; Where
Am I Going
(EP) Philips BE12605

Dusty Springfield: Twenty-Four Hours From Tulsa; Anyone Who
Had A Heart; Go Ahead On; Every Day I Have To Cry; Now
That You're My Baby; The Corrupt Ones; The Look Of Love;
Live It Up; I Wish I'd Never Loved You; Reste encore un instant;
Who Can I Turn To; I Want Your Love Tonight
(LP) World Record Club T848

I Will Come To You/ The Colour Of Your Eyes
Philips BF1706

Dusty Definitely: Ain't No Sun Since You've Been Gone; Take
Another Little Piece Of My Heart; Another Night; Mr Dream
Merchant; I Can't Give Back The Love I Feel For You; Love
Power; This Girl's In Love With You; I Only Want To Laugh;

Who Will Take My Place; I Think It's Gonna Rain Today;
Morning; Second Time Around
(LP) Philips SBL7864

Son Of A Preacher Man/ Just A Little Lovin'
Philips BF1730

Stay Awhile: I Only Want To Be With You; Stay Awhile; Mama
Said; Anyone Who Had A Heart; When The Lovelight Starts
Shining Thru His Eyes; Wishin' & Hopin'; Mockingbird; You
Don't Own Me; Something Special; Every Day I Have To Cry
(LP) Wing WL1211

1969
Dusty In Memphis: Just A Little Lovin'; So Much Love; Son Of
A Preacher Man; I Don't Want To Hear It Any More; Don't
Forget About Me; Breakfast In Bed; Just One Smile; The
Windmills Of Your Mind; In The Land Of Make Believe; No
Easy Way Down; I Can't Make It Alone
(LP) Philips SBL7889

Am I The Same Girl/ Earthbound Girl
Philips BF1811

Brand New Me/ Bad Case Of The Blues
Philips BF1826

1970 (recorded 1969)
From Dusty....With Love: Lost; Bad Case Of The Blues; Never
Love Again; Let Me Get In Your Way; Let's Get Together Soon;
Brand New Me; Joe; Silly Fool; The Star Of My Show; Let's
Talk It Over
(LP) Philips SBL7927

Helen Shapiro

Teenager Sings The Blues

M any regarded her as something of a novelty, a flash in the pan. She was certainly much more than that, though her chart life was fairly brief: hitting the dizzy heights of success in 1961, she enjoyed two chart-toppers and eight Top 40 hits. Three years later, her commercial career was all but over—much less to do with lack of talent, which she possessed in bundles, than in the direction the British music scene was taking with the advent of Mersey Mania. Had she emerged a little later, she might have achieved the same level of long-lasting fame as a Cilla or a Dusty.

The descendent of Russian Jewish immigrants who had settled in London's East End, Helen Shapiro was born at the Bethnal Green Hospital on 28 September 1946. Hers was a musical family: her mother, Rachel, played the violin and her father, Barney, is said to have been possessed of a fine singing voice. The Shapiros—grandparents, aunts and uncles, cousins— all lived within a few streets of each other. Most were involved with the tailoring business and, though far from wealthy, appear to have been a happy and contented group who worked hard and who, like most close-knit Jewish families, frequently got together once the shutters came down for a good old-fashioned shindig. The religious festivals were especially exciting because these brought in relatives from further afield. No one possessed a record player, and aside from the wireless this was their main source of entertainment. Helen's favourites in these days were stalwarts Bing Crosby, Doris Day and Rosemary Clooney, along with Jewish institutions Al Jolson and Sophie Tucker. "I have fond memories of my childhood," she recalled, "Nobody ever had the chance to get big-headed. It was drilled into us from a very early age that musical talent was a gift from God. In a family so talented, who were we to argue?"

Helen had an older brother, Ronnie (born 1942) with whom she shared a room in the cramped upper storey of a terraced house in Reighton Road, Upper Clapton. There were no facilities, so if anyone wanted to take a bath they had to drag out the tin tub and fill it from the copper boiler in the kitchen—otherwise it meant taking a trip to the public baths in nearby Hackney. At five, Helen was enrolled at Northwood Road School where, from a tender age, she learned to cope with anti-Semitism: the establishment was in the heart of the Jewish community, with around a quarter of the pupils belonging to the faith, so she never felt isolated. At seven, she joined the Clapton Jewish Youth Club: Ronnie was already a member, and music was frequently on the agenda. Then in 1955 the Shapiros moved to a maisonette in Hackney's Rutland Road: this had three bedrooms so that Helen no longer had to share, a bathroom, and a small garden. Within walking distance was a cinema where she and her mother would watch the latest Hollywood musicals. She had already made up her mind that she wanted to be a singer. Also, by now her taste in music had changed: she was into Bill Haley, Elvis Presley, Neil Sedaka—and Cliff Richard, who later became a friend. Sometimes she and her pals would hang around outside the stage door of the Hackney Empire. Her proudest moment in those days, she said, was getting Marty Wilde's autograph.

In 1957, Helen, her brother and a group of friends from the youth club—one was lorry driver's son Mark Feld, who later became Marc Bolan—formed their own band. Their repertoire comprised the chart hits of the day, but with an emphasis on skiffle. Helen also developed a passion for entering talent contests, whenever she and her family went to Westcliff or Margate—invariably walking off with first prize. When skiffle started to go out of fashion, she and Ronnie turned to jazz—her field of expertise today. How she came about her unusual voice—basso profundo, even at the age of eleven—is a matter for conjecture, most likely a combination of ancestry and very early smoking. She confesses in her memoirs that, at junior school, she liked nothing more than sneaking into the playground toilets to light up.

Helen's quest for fame came courtesy of her Uncle Harry, who saw an ad in the local paper for the grandly-titled Maurice Burman School of Pop Singing. Burman, whose offices were in Bickenhall Mansions, at the junction of Baker Street and Marylbone Road, had been a drummer with Geraldo's orchestra during World War II. Besides running his academy he wrote a column for *Melody Maker*. His fees—25 shillings for four hours tuition on Saturday mornings—were steep, but if the talent was there his success rate was high. He had helped Alma Cogan when she had been starting out.

Helen had been with Burman's academy for a month before she met the man himself. Burman was so impressed with her raw, as yet untrained talent that when Uncle Harry—paying for the lessons—asked how she was shaping up, Burman informed him that from now on her fee would be wavered because, in his estimation, she had already reached the point where she should be considered for a recording contract. A few days later, Helen auditioned for John Barry, who had written for Adam Faith and would later compose for the Bond movies. Barry knocked her back, but not to be outdone, Burman encouraged her to continue with her lessons.

A few months later, Helen was placed under the tutelage of John Schroeder, then assistant to the conductor Norrie Paramor, who doubled as A & R executive producer for Columbia

Records. Paramor (1914-79), a former MD with Ralph Reader's Gang Show and pianist with Harrie Gold, will go down in history for producing a wide range of number one singles and albums. Figuring among his greatest successes were Ruby Murray ("Softly, Soflty"), Michael Holliday ("The Story Of My Life"), Eddie Calvert ("Oh Mein Papa"), Cliff Richard ("Living Doll") and Amália Rodrigues (*On Broadway*).

Schroeder auditioned Helen at Abbey Road. She put her heart and soul into "Birth Of The Blues", as would later happen when she recorded the piece, and Schroeder later observed, "She had a very jazzy voice, very deep, like a boy. Her timing, her phrasing and her whole presence was extremely strong—right in your face, I couldn't believe it!" Schroeder played the acetate to Norrie Paramor, who also thought she was a boy. Helen sang for him, and was told that an initial six-months recording contract was hers for the taking. The only condition was that, as a minor, her parents would have to sign on her behalf.

For five of these months, Columbia deliberated over Helen's debut single, until finally they had to let her record something, or let her go. Commercially, she was an "in-between"—too young for romantic ballads in the stamp of Joan Regan or Petula Clark, yet too mature for juvenile ditties. Neither did they want her to cover an American pop song of ,which there was glut. Paramor decided that something topical would have to be written especially for her, and gave the job to John Schroeder, who joined forces with Mike Hawker. The result was "Don't Treat Me Like A Child"—a good song, marred only by the squeaky "*yeah-yeahs*" of the female backing singers. To create a gimmick, though she was very much against the idea, Helen was photographed in her school uniform—strumming a banjo. The song and the record's flipside, Maurice Burman's catchy "When I'm With You", were recorded at Abbey Road with session musicians from the Ted Heath Band—both tracks, like most of Helen's future recordings (which makes her almost unique in Brit pop) were laid down in a single take. "I didn't get nervous," she recalled, "I just did what I knew how to do. Mum and Dad probably felt more nervous than I did."

Helen cut the record in January 1961, and it was rush-released the following month. The Shapiros still did not own a record player—a problem which would soon be solved by the ever-benevolent Uncle Harry—so in order to listen to it, everyone had to nip around to a neighbour's house. Helen then resumed her "normal" life—school, and swotting for her exams. Life, of course, would never be the same again. "Don't Treat Me Like A Child" entered the charts, stalled at Number 28, then dropped out. Early in May, she was invited to appear on the pilot of television's *Thank Your Lucky Stars*: topping the bill was Michael Holliday. Introduced by Keith Fordyce, and with no other song to offer, she performed this one. Within a week it had re-entered the charts, and this time shot to Number 3. Suddenly, Britain had a new major talent, though Helen did not feel much like celebrating. That same week, her mentor Maurice Burman succumbed to cancer.

Burman's much younger widow, Jean, and Norrie Paramor's brother Alan now took over the handling of Helen's career. Jean taught her the rudimentaries of presentation—how to dress and apply make-up, how to move on stage and rid herself of the wooden stance one sees in her early filmed performances. Paramor took care of her engagements which, with her still attending school, were for now restricted to weekends and holidays.

These early shows saw her emulating Alma Cogan's dress style—hooped skirts, under which she wore yards and yards of tulle. Away from the spotlight, she liked to dress like any fashionable young woman—sloppy-joe pullovers, slacks or tight skirts, and winkle-picker shoes. She was promoted as "The British Brenda Lee", quite simply because Columbia had no one else to compare her with. She was of course nothing like Brenda Lee—or Connie Francis, the only other female singer in the charts while "Don't Treat Me Like A Child" was in the Top Ten, with whom comparisons were also made. Then for a little while, the press awarded her the somewhat unflattering monicker, "Foghorn". This was how she was affectionately known by her youth club bandmates, though the tabloids used it only as a form of derision.

Unlike any other pop star who had enjoyed a major hit, Helen's schoolgirl status prevented her from doing much in the way of live performances. She was permitted to sing on Radio Luxembourg's *EMI Spectaculars*, hosted by Muriel Young and broadcast during the early evening. The BBC only had it's Light Programme in those days, and Luxembourg was the only station which played "young" music. The press, once they discovered that Helen was not a boy, made endless comparisons with Cliff Richard, claiming that she looked like him—in early photographs, the resemblance is uncanny. She met all her pop heroes—Cliff, Bobby Vee, Frank Ifield, Adam Faith—but confessed to having crushes on stars she had yet to meet, such as Paul Anka and Paul Newman. At fifteen she had a regular boyfriend, but the promoters at Columbia asked her to keep the romance low-key. It remained so until they split up, whence the tabloids made up the story that her parents had brought it to a halt. Away from the television, radio or recording studio, Helen tried to live her life as she had before fame beckoned—still going to the youth club once a week, or relaxing at home with her family.

Helen's second single was John Schroeder and Mike Hawker's "You Don't Know", an engaging exercise in teenage angst and completely different from its predecessor. Simply but effectively orchestrated by Martin Slavin, and containing its fair share of "*woah-woah-woahs*" this time, it topped the charts for three weeks in the late autumn of 1961. It remained in the Top 40 for five months—making Helen, at 14 years and 316 days, the youngest ever female artiste to have had a Number One—though the youngest, per se, had been Frankie Lymon, one year younger than Helen when his "Why Do Fools Fall In Love" had topped the UK charts in 1956. Interestingly, the youngest ever star to top the *Billboard* chart (also in 1956) had also been British, and ironically from Bethnall Green—14-year-old Laurie London, with his only hit, "He's Got The Whole World In His Hands". On the flipside of Helen's record, which sold 500,000 copies and earned her her first Silver Disc, Columbia had plumped for Norrie Paramor and drag-queen Bunny Lewis's excellent, "Marvellous Lie", which if anything was *better* than the A-side.

Suddenly, Helen was appearing in all the big television pop shows of the day—*Oh, Boy!*, *Thank Your Lucky Stars*, and *Juke Box Jury*—and making live appearances with The Shadows, Joe Brown, The Tremeloes, and The Temperance Seven. Almost always she was promoted as top of the bill, but because of her age not permitted to work Sundays, or close the show because of the 10 pm curfew imposed by the entertainment rules of the day. Foreign tours meant that she had to be chaperoned—in Europe by her mother, further afield by both parents. Her biggest engagement saw her supporting Dorothy Squires at Chester's Royalty Theatre. "We were told to expect this archetypal little Shirley Temple prima donna," Dorothy told me, "But she was such a sweet little thing, polite, well aware of what she wanted out of her career, and so tremendously talented. I adored her!"

Helen's third single, released in September 1961 is the song which will always be most associated with her—annoyingly so, she has said (though in 1993 she would use the title for her memoirs) in that some think it to have been the *only* song she ever sang. "Walkin' Back To Happiness", written by her by now regular team of Schroeder and Hawker, subsequently won them an Ivor Novello Award, yet initially she disliked it. "It reminded me of 'Campdown races'," she recalled, adding that she had much preferred the B-side, Norrie Paramor's rhythm and blues-stype "Kiss N Run". The "*woah-woah-woahs*" were now replaced by "*woopah-oh-yeah-yeahs*", and this one topped the charts for three weeks before being toppled by Elvis Presley's "Little Sister". Much was expected of the American release, but the record only reached a disappointing Number 100 in the *Billboard* chart. While it was riding high in the British charts, Helen celebrated her fifteenth birthday at London's Talk of the

Town—not performing, but as a guest at Dorothy Squires' opening night as the first ever British act to top the bill there.

Soon afterwards, Helen left school, and a few weeks later topped the bill on television's *Sunday Night At The London Palladium*. In November, she flew to Paris where she performed two songs in the first half of the Georges Brassens show at the Olympia. "You Don't Know" had proved a hit in France, and "Walkin' Back To Happiness" had just entered the French Top 40. She also recorded the song phonetically in German, and topped the charts with it in Japan. Later, she would successfully tour Australasia, South Africa, Israel, and make a lightning trip to New York where she appeared on Ed Sullivan's *Toast Of The Town*—an experience she claimed she had hated because of the host's rudeness and condescending attitude towards some of his guests. There would also be a two-weeks season at the Palladium with Matt Monroe, whilst *Melody Maker* named her Top British Female Vocalist. The Variety Club of Great Britain awarded her their Silver Heart for Most Promising Newcomer. For a couple of years, Helen Shapiro was sitting on top of the world.

Helen's next single, released in February 1962, was Jeff Barry's "Tell Me What He Said", c/w "I Apologise", which reached Number 2 in the charts—her friends, The Shadows, kept her from the top spot with "Wonderful Land". Barry's "Tell Laura I Love Her" had given Ricky Valance a British chart-topper. Next up was Norrie Paramor and Bunny Lewis's "Let's Talk About Love", so short that it is almost over as soon as it begins—this reached a disappointing but hardly surprising Number 23 in the charts. Helen sang it in the film, *It's Trad, Dad!*, of which the least said the better. Directed by Richard (*Superman*) Lester, this also featured Craig Douglas, Gene Vincent, and Chubby Checker. Everyone played themselves in a scenario which sees a young couple campaigning to introduce the trad-jazz fad into their neighbourhood, when the oldies do not want it.

There would be an even worse follow-up movie, *Play It Cool*, directed by Michael Winner. Featuring Billy Fury, playing a character called Billy Universe, the singing was great but the acting dire. Helen performed two songs: "I Don't Care" and "Cry My Heart Out". The former appeared on the flipside of Schroeder and Hawker's stunning teen-angst ballad, "Little Miss Lonely", her penultimate single of 1962, and which peaked at Number 8 in the charts—the latter song on the flipside of its successor, the raunchy "Keep Away From Other Girls" The fans kept away from the record, which barely scraped into the Top 40. Almost certainly this would not had happened had she recorded it a few years later, for its composer was the then little-known Burt Bacharach. Columbia had also scrapped the original demo which contained lyrics which see the impressionable girl criticising the smooth-talking seducer who has wooed her with, "A hero sandwich and a glass of wine—a smile, a smoke, and oh such a great big line!" It was not considered appropriate for a teenage girl to advocate smoking, though Helen was fond of her tobacco, therefore "smoke" was substituted by "joke".

Helen was singing better than ever, and releasing records of supreme quality—Artie Wayne and Ben Raleigh's "Queen For Tonight" was one of her best songs of 1963, and almost made the Top Thirty—but as the new year dawned, commercially it would all be downhill aside from "No Trespassing", which topped the Australian charts. Her albums, excellent as these were, followed the same pattern, the exception being her first one, *Tops With Me*, released in 1962. This reached Number 2—a few hundred copies more and it would have occupied the top spot. It's successors, including *Helen's Sixteen* (the title was two-fold, sixteen tracks to coincide with her sixteenth birthday), and *Helen Hits Out!* did not chart, but contained some pretty eclectic material—there was a near-definitive version of "Basin Street Blues" ultimately proving that jazz would always be Helen's first love.

Tops For Me was Columbia—and Helen—demonstrating her sheer versatilty, for it is representative of several very distinctive styles: pop, rock, chanson, jazz and blues. There is The Shirelles' "Will You Love Me Tomorrow?—less strident and slower-paced than the original; a more than competent version of Elvis's "Are

You Lonesome Tonight?"; a not so good one of Marty Wilde's "Teenager In Love"—by now, the teen-angst theme was starting to wear thin. From the French catalogue there was Gilbert Bécaud's "The Day The Rains Came" (Le jour ou la pluie viendra) and Charles Trenet's "Beyond The Sea" (La mer). Helen's stab at Connie Francis's "Lipstick On Your Collar" and Brenda Lee's "Sweet Nothin's" are way above average, and her take on Marv Johnson's "You've Got What It Takes" may well be the first ever British cover of a Motown song.

At the end of 1962 Helen hit the road again, with The Beatles third on in a six-act bill and performing just four songs. The nationwide tour ticked off in Bradford, with Helen topping the bill and by now and actually staying to close the show. Within a few weeks, however, their roles were reversed when the group's "Please Please Me" rocketed to Number 2 in the charts. Suddenly, in a strange twist of fate, The Beatles became all the rage and Helen was shunted aside—though she might not have slipped out of the charts so expediently had Columbia allowed her to record "Misery", the song Lennon and McCartney penned for her at the time. Such a title, the company declared, was wholly unsuited for a teenager and the number was given to Kenny Lynch.

Helen's record sales plummeted in the aftermath of this tour. "I'd been a novelty at fourteen but suffered from the Shirley Temple syndrome," she recalled, "I'd grown up. Suddenly I was beginning to look a bit passé in spite of topping the bill." The quality of her material, on the other hand, only seemed to get better. In 1963, the year she ended her hugely successful run with Columbia, she pre-empted Dusty by proving that the likes of Dionne Warwick did not have a monolopy on Motown—many believe Helen's version of "Walk On By" to have been far classier than Warwick's, and another gem was Berry Gordy's "Shop Around". Equally stunning was her cover of Carole King's "It Might As Well Rain Until September". The best interpretation of all, however, would come in 1964 with her sassy cover version of Doris Day's "Move Over Darling"—sexy and daring at the time for a 17-year-old promoted as the archetypal wholesome girl-next-door. Also ahead of Dusty, and sadly just as unsuccessful despite the contribution of legendary saxophonist Boots Randolph, was Helen's Stateside-recorded album, *Helen In Nashville*—her cover of Jackie DeShannon's "Woe Is Me", taken from this, entered the *Billboard* Top 30, though the album itself failed to make much of an impression. Another great song on this album was "It's My Party". This track was pencilled in for Helen's next single release, but Columbia deliberated over it for so long that Mercury Records gazumped them and released the version by the then unknown Lesley Gore. The so-called "brat song", produced by Quincy Jones and which gave the youth of America their latest buzz phrase, "It's my party, and I'll cry if I want to," topped the US charts and reached Number 9 in Britain.

Throughout the mid-Sixties, Helen continued touring home and abroad, travelling off the (then) beaten track as far afield as Poland and the Eastern bloc, Hong Kong, and the Philippines. She appeared regularly in pantomime and turned her attention to stage musicals. Her passion for jazz saw her championed by such legends as Humphrey Lyttleton. Still only eighteen, she was shortlisted to play Fanny Brice in the London production of *Funny Girl*, and doubtless would have excelled in the role—this was subsequently given to its creator, Barbra Streisand. At the end of 1969, Helen sang "Walkin' Back To Happiness" in the BBC's *Pop Go The Sixties*. Appearing with her were fellow Brit Girls Dusty, Cilla Black, Sandie Shaw, and Lulu.

Following appearances in several smaller theatrical productions, in 1979 Helen was cast in the role of Nancy— originally played by Georgia Brown—in the revival of Lionel Bart's *Oliver!* This played to capacity audiences in London's West End for almost a year. The reviews were excellent—only the acid-tongued Jean Rook, for whom few could do right, found fault with her performance, denouncing her voice as sounding "like a docker with laryngitis". She also appeared in Willy Russell's adult comedy, *One For The Road*, and played Cynthia Lennon in television's surreal drama about the murdered Beatle,

A Journey In The Life. This same year, 1985, she was cast as hairdresser Viv Harker in Granada TV's twice-weekly soap, *Albion Market*. Arguably one of her biggest mistakes was accepting the part of Fantine in *Les Miserable*, only to back out of the production at the last minute because she was moving home!

Helen's personal life has not always been so successful. In 1967, following a whirlwind courtship, she married the promoter Duncan C Weldon, five years her senior—this coincided with the release of a single, "She Needs Company". Her parents did not attend the ceremony: Weldon's father was Jewish, his mother so only by conversion to Judaism. The marriage lasted just a few years. In 1971, Helen wed clothing manufacturer Morris Gundlash—this one lasted a little longer. She is currently married to the actor John Judd, who she met while appearing in *Cabaret* in Lancaster. She has never had children.

In 1987, Helen became a Messianic Jew—one who believes in Christ as the Messiah. As such she has recorded several Messianic albums and, like her friend Cliff Richard, has toured with her own gospel show. "I could never understand why Christians often looked so miserable and po-faced," she said of her new faith, "The black churches had the right idea. Their choirs and congregations looked as if they were *enjoying* their worship!"

And what, after half a century in the business, does Helen Shapiro regard as her greatest achievement in life? Her music? Her marriage? No, it is this latent religious revelation which she describes as, "More important than the day I went to Maurice Burnam's school of pop singing, far more important than getting to Number One in the charts or appearing at the London Palladium, even more important than playing Nancy or making jazz records!"

Helen Shapiro

Discography: Top 50 Vinyl

1961
Don't Treat Me Like A Child/ When I'm With You
Columbia DB4589

You Don't Know/ Marvellous Lie
Columbia DB4670

Walkin' Back To Happiness/ Kiss N Run
Columbia DB4715

1962
Tell Me What He Said/ I Apologise
Columbia DB4782

Helen: Goody Goody; The Birth Of The Blues; Tiptoe Through
The Tulips; After You've Gone
(EP) Columbia SEG8128

Let's Talk About Love/ Sometime Yesterday

Helen Shapiro's Hit Parade: Don't Treat Me Like A Child; You Don't Know; Walkin' Back To Happiness; When I'm With You (EP) Columbia SEG8136

Little Miss Lonely/ I Don't Care
Columbia DB4869

'Tops' With Me: Little Devil; Will You Love Me Tomorrow; Because They're Young; The Day The Rains Came; Are You Lonesome Tonight; Teenager In Love; Lipstick On Your Collar; Beyond The Sea; Sweet Nothin's; You Mean Everything To Me; I Love You; You Got What It Takes
(LP) Columbia 33SX 1397/ SCX 3428

Keep Away From Other Girls/ Cry My Heart Out
Columbia DB4908

1963
Queen For Tonight/ Daddy Couldn't Get Me One Of Those
Columbia DB4966

Woe Is Me/ I Walked Right In
Columbia DB7206

Not Responsible/ No Trespassing
Columbia DB7072 (#1, Australia)

Look Who It Is/ Walking In My Dreams
Columbia DB7130

1964
Fever/ Ole Father Time
Columbia DB7190

Bibliography

Bret, David: Interviews with Marlene Dietrich & Kris Kirk

Coleman, Ray: Interview with DS, *London Evening Standard*, 1970

Davis, Sharon: *Dusty: An Intimate Portrait*, Sevenoaks, 2008

Evans, David: *Scissors & Paste: A Collage Biography of Dusty Springfield*, Britannia Press, 1995

Howes, Paul: *The Complete Dusty Springfield* (Reynolds & Hearn, 2001)

Kirk, Kris: Interview with DS: *A Boy Called Mary*, Millivres, 1999

O'Brien, Lucy: *Dusty* (Sidgwick & Jackson, 1989)

Shapiro, Helen: *Walking Back To Happiness*, Harper Collins, 1993

Rook, Jean: Interview with DS, *Daily Express*, 1985

Valentine, Penny; Wickham, Vicki: *Dusty Springfield: Dancing With Demons*, Hodder & Stoughton, 2000

About The Author

D avid Bret was born in Paris in November 1954. Regarded as Britain's leading authority on the French *chanson*, his acclaimed books include biographies of Edith Piaf, Maurice Chevalier, Mistinguett, Marlene Dietrich, Morrissey, Maria Callas, Tallulah Bankhead, Barbra Streisand, Rock Hudson, Clark Gable, Rudolph Valentino, Jean Harlow, Mario Lanza, Joan Crawford, Freddie Mercury, Gracie Fields, Nick Drake, Jeff Buckley, Gram Parsons and George Formby. Additionally he has made over 600 radio broadcasts, and a dozen television documentaries in Britain, Europe and the United States.

1182591R0

Printed in Great Britain by
Amazon.co.uk, Ltd.,
Marston Gate.